The World of
Karl Pilkington

Ricky Gervais
presents

The World of Karl Pilkington

by
Ricky Gervais, Stephen Merchant and Karl Pilkington

All drawings by
Karl Pilkington

NEW YORK

ISBN-10:   1-4013-0342-0
ISBN-13:   978-14013-0342-6

Hyperion books are available for special promotions and premiums. For details contact Michael Rentas, Assistant Director, Inventory Operations, Hyperion, 77 West 66th Street, 11th floor, New York, New York 10023, or call 212-456-0133.

Cover photograph and design by Glyn Hughes

FIRST EDITION

10 9 8 7 6 5 4 3 2 1

For Suzanne, Mum and Dad

Foreword

How is it that a man who holds the beliefs that 'the Chinese don't age well' and that 'gays go out too late' can be so likeable?

Because he's an idiot.

He says what he thinks without malice – it's just that he doesn't think before he says it.

Received wisdom says there's a fine line between a genius and an idiot. Not true. Karl's an idiot, plain and simple. Very simple. Some people have proclaimed him a genius, but they're idiots.

I first met Karl when Steve and I were hosting a radio show. We needed someone to press the buttons and they gave us Karl. The first time he opened his mouth it was like we'd discovered a magic lamp. If you rubbed it, magical twaddle came out. (I never rubbed it, although I did squeeze its head in between records. It was the roundest head I'd ever seen and still is.)

This book contains some of the beliefs and theories that have cropped up in conversations between myself, Steve Merchant and Karl over the years.

Is Karl an idiot? I'll keep out of it. You make your own mind up.

But if you think he's a genius, you're an idiot.

Ricky Gervais
London, June 2006
www.rickygervais.com

Karl by Ricky

'Must of nicked it from somewhere.'

Steve: What do you make of the first genetically modified baby? Are you worried about this?

Karl: Do you know what they do?

Ricky: Isn't it just choosing the eye colour or something?

Steve: Well this is the concern, isn't it, that in the future you will be able to decide whether it's a boy or a girl, how intelligent it is, what it looks like, is it handsome, is it ugly? Obviously no one would choose an ugly baby and so on and so on. So where will it end? Are you concerned?

Karl: We've talked about the cloning thing a bit before, ain't we, and how it's a bit weird?

Ricky: Yes.

Karl: I don't think it matters because at the end of the day you might look like some other kid but it's the way that you're brought up that will change your features and your personality.

1

Ricky: If you lie you get a long nose, don't you?

Karl: No, but listen, right, 'cos I remember when I was growing up on the estate ...

Ricky: This is gonna be good.

Karl: So I'm growing up on this estate and there was this woman about four houses down who was a bit rough.

Ricky: Go on ...

Karl: They didn't clean up much right, and even if you haven't got a lot of money you can still try and make the place look nice.

Ricky: Get some Jif, yeah.

Karl: Right, but she didn't. Her kid used to take a horse into the house.

Ricky: Sorry?

Steve: Woah woah woah.

Ricky: Woah, Neddy, woah. What do you mean, 'her kid used to take a horse into the house'? Where did they get the horse?

Karl: Must of nicked it from somewhere.

Steve: What, from outside the saloon round the corner?

Ricky: Did 'Big Jake' come looking for it?

Steve: So let me get this right. Was this before the lynching or after?

Ricky: Where did he get a horse from? What do you mean, 'he must of nicked it'? His mum is saying, 'Where did you get that from?', he says, 'I've bought it', she goes, 'Oh alright then, but keep it out of the kitchen.'

Steve: 'And I don't want you going cattle rustling ...'

Ricky: Where did he get a horse from and how long did he have it for? Was he leading it or riding it? 'Mam, quick, open the door, I can't stop, looks like we've got us a runaway ...' What do you mean?

Karl: I'm just saying I don't think they could of afforded to buy one 'cos they're not cheap, so I'm just guessing. Maybe that's wrong of me.

Steve: He had a horse! That's why the family didn't have any money. They had a horse!

Karl: I was in the car with me dad coming into the avenue and he used to have to drive down it to turn round ...

Ricky: You had the traditional method of transport.

Karl: ... And the horse was in the lounge. And I went in there once because I tried to earn myself some money by flogging little flowers in plastic cups.

Ricky: This is genius, it just keeps coming. What do you mean, 'you tried flogging little flowers'? This story is getting deeper and deeper. It's like an onion.

Steve: We've created a whole world here where there's a man living with a horse. I come from the West Country and I never heard anything like that.

Ricky: I just think of a big orange carpet, a Rediffusion telly and this horse going, 'I'm fed up in here'

Steve: Exactly, saying, 'I am not taking the rubbish out again.'

Ricky: Little flowers in pots? What do you mean? Let's just go back. What did this woman look like?

Karl: Er ... bit like – and no disrespect to her – bit like Pauline Quirke.

Steve: Sure.

Karl: They did this thing at school about raising money for some local charity and they said you can do anything to raise money and they came up with all these ideas. And I thought, 'That's good. Forget the charity. I'm the charity.' So I asked me mam for some flowers 'cos she had a lot of 'em around the house. I said, 'Can I just take some snippings of them and I'll go and buy some plastic cups and get some soil out of the garden'. Planted the bits of plants in them, got a tray, had about 25 plants on it, selling 'em for around 25 pence each. Sold loads.

Ricky: You didn't just cut the flowers off and stick them in the pots?

Karl: Yeah, they wouldn't of survived. But I think people sort of thought, 'good on him for trying'. But anyway, I went round to the house with the horse 'cos I thought their house could do with a bit of colour and brightening up and that.

Ricky: The horse went, 'Thank God for that – breakfast! They've been feeding me Kit-e-kat.'

Karl: So I go up to the door and they open the door and it's one of them houses where there's no carpet ...

Steve: And a horse in the living room. We've all been there.

Karl: And the horse was walking round the living room. And it looked quite happy and everything because ...

Ricky: *Black Beauty* was on?

Karl: But think about it right; if you were a horse, where would you rather be? In a little wooden hut with a load of hay? Or in a house with a three-piece suite and a telly and that?

Ricky: A telly and that.

Karl: I was saying this the other day. I was walking through London the other day with Suzanne and do you know how homeless people always have dogs? She said, 'Oh I hope they look after it' and I said, 'What you on about? That dog is happier than most dogs because people always walk past and give it a pat on the head; it's with its owner all the time; it's out in the open not locked up in the house.'

Steve: 'It doesn't eat, but other than that ...'

Karl: No it does eat. They're always alright. So that's what
        I was saying, I think this horse was doing alright for
        itself.

Ricky: Well, yes, not many horses have got their own house
        for a start.

Karl: But anyway, that's not what we were talking about.
        We were talking about ...

Steve: ... Genetically modified kids.

Karl: Yeah. What I'm saying is, you could have a baby,
        right, Steve, and Ricky could see it and say, 'God, I
        want one that looks like that.'

Steve: It could happen Rick, come on, work with him.

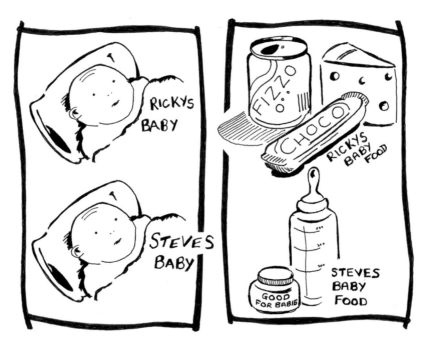

Karl: So you take it to the doctors and ... I don't know what they do with it, they inject it with summit or whatever ...

Steve: Yep, that's how it's done.

Karl: And you get a little baby and there it is – it looks the same. Now you both go off and do your own things, right. Steve, you look after your baby, you treat it well, you give it good food and that.

Steve: Yes, well I'm a good dad.

Karl: But Ricky just gives his cheese. So it changes its looks, it goes a bit fat, it gets tired easily. Now this family ...

Ricky: Why am I just feeding a baby cheese?

Karl: Now this family who had a horse in the house, they had a little baby and me mam went round and came back and said, 'You're not gonna believe this but it's a beautiful little baby.' And the weird thing was it was a good looking kid but as time went on they didn't really look after it – I'm not saying they abused it – but it used to run around and play out 'til ten at night, it used to chase cars ...

Steve: Right. Did it have hooves?

Ricky: It used to chase cars? What sort of kid chases cars? Was it called 'Rover'? Did it fetch sticks?

Karl: The weird thing is, it was a good looking kid but as time went on and all that not eating properly, its hair was all patchy and it became an ugly kid. And that's what I'm saying, right; you can clone all you like but at the end of the day, it's how you're brought up.

Steve: Man alive, that was one hell of a point.

Karl: But am I right?

Ricky: Er ... you're always right, Karl.

PETS

THERE ARE LOADS OF PETS NOW, YEARS AGO YOU HAD THE CHOICE OF A CAT OR A DOG BUT NOW PEOPLE HAVE SPIDERS, SNAKES, TORTOISE AND GERBILS. I HAD A MAGPIE FOR A BIT. IT LANDED ON ME BIKE ONE DAY AND JUST HUNG ABOUT.
AFTER A FEW MONTHS IT GOT NASTY FOR SOME REASON. IT STARTED PECKING ME HEAD AND POPPED THE TYRES ON ME GRIFTER. ME MAM SAID IT GOT NASTY COS OF THE TOFFEES I WAS FEEDING IT. I GOT RID OF IT IN THE END BY CYCLING FOR MILES AND PUSHING IT OFF MY BIKE THEN CYCLED AWAY.

MAGGIE

FLUFFY

FLUFFY WAS A DOG WE GOT HANDED DOWN TO US WHEN ME MAMS MAM DIED. IT WAS A KIND OF POODLE. IT NEVER REALLY SETTLED BEING WITH US. ME MAMS MAM USED TO SPOIL IT AND TREAT IT LIKE A HUMAN. WE THINK SHE USED TO WATCH CORONATION STREET WITH IT COS EVERYTIME IT HEARD THE THEME TUNE IT STARTED CRYING. THIS GOT DEPRESSING COS CORONATION STREET WAS ON 4 TIMES A WEEK. IT GOT HIT BY A CAR WHEN WE LET IT OUT, ME MAM SAID IT TRIED TO KILL ITSELF COS IT WAS MISSING ME MAMS MAM.
AFTER THE ACCIDENT IT USED TO RUN SIDEWAYS LIKE A CRAB.

RICKY'S LIZARD THING

RICKYS GOT A PET THAT PEOPLE SHOULDNT HAVE, ITS SOME SORT OF LIZARD THING. IT DOESNT DO ANYTHING, THE PICTURE IVE DONE OF IT IS PROBABLY MORE ACTIVE, HE MAY ASWELL HAVE AN ORNAMENT IN THE CAGE.
HE HAS TO BUY IT LIVE CRICKETS FOR ITS FOOD WHICH IS WEIRD COS THE FOOD IT EATS IS MORE INTERESTING TO WATCH THAN THE PET LIZARD IS.

FISH

PETS THAT YOU CAN'T HOLD OR STROKE ARN'T WORTH HAVING. SUZANNE ME GIRLFRIEND WANTS A FISH BUT IVE TOLD HER IT AINT WORTH IT.
IVE TOLD HER SHE MIGHT ASWELL HAVE ONE OF THEM FISH SCREENSAVERS... THEY LOOK AS REAL AND YOU DONT HAVE TO FEED EM.

'Look, if you don't wanna do it, we won't do it!'

Karl: No, but my thing with iPods is – do we need 'em? We're living in that era now where we've invented most of the stuff that we need, and now we're just messing about.

Ricky: They said that in 1900. Someone actually said, 'Everything to be invented has already been invented.' They said that in 1900, and how wrong were they?

Karl: No, but what did they invent in 1900 that made 'em go, 'We've done it all now?'

Ricky: Well think what happened in the twentieth century.

Karl: Go on.

Ricky: Cars, planes.

Karl: Yeah, but is that a good thing, planes and that? Do you need a plane really? Wouldn't it have been better if we were all stuck where we should be, instead of travelling about?

Ricky: Why?

Karl: War. War's happening innit, because everyone's saying, 'Well now we can fly, we'll go over there and invade that lot.'

Steve: So there were no wars prior to the invention of the aeroplane?

Karl: Not like there is today. What I'm saying is, the world has got smaller, hasn't it? Everyone is saying that. I was saying to you the other day how we now go to places where we shouldn't go. People go on holiday to places where you've got to have an injection before you go there. Forget it then. That's a warning. Don't go there!

Ricky: I am with you on that. I don't want to enter a country where I have to have an injection to stop me from dying while I am in that country. I totally agree with you on that.

Karl: So what happened is, so they invented a plane and it's like, 'Oh let's go on holiday' and then they go, 'You'll die though', 'Oh, well you've got to invent summit.' 'Let's invent an injection' and then it's like 'Right, what else do we need to go to that place?' There's a lot of faffing.

Steve and Ricky laugh.

Karl: What I'm saying is, you know Steve's travelled more than I have. You've been to, like, dangerous places.

Steve: I have been to places where you need injections, yeah.

Karl: Yeah but why?

Steve: Because it's fascinating. Do you not believe in the idea that travel broadens the mind? It makes you experience other ways of life, other ways of thinking. It enriches you as a human being. That's the whole reason people go travelling.

Karl: But since the invention of the telly you don't have to go that far.

Steve: You're absolutely right.

Ricky: So there you go then. The telly was invented in the twentieth century wasn't it?

Karl: Yeah, it's pretty good.

Steve: Where would you stop then? Would you stop inventing stuff right now or do you think we could carry on for another five years – see what comes up and then just draw a line under it all?

Karl: We are just messing about.

Ricky: But there's still things to do – a cure for cancer, a cure for AIDS.

Karl: Yeah but should we mess with that?

Ricky: What d'you mean?

Karl: Because there's too many people in the world as it is, in't there? So that's a way of controlling it. You know, look at London, right, it's over-populated. Rent keeps going up because there's more and more people surviving. If you let 'em die, it's gonna even itself out. I was saying to someone the other day about maybe we should look at – if we are going to invent something – forget like the traditional way of people having kids, right, the way they have it away and that, you know ...

Ricky: What do you mean?

Karl: You know, the way that we have kids and stuff. It'd be good if what happened was, to control it, a man and woman, right, they're born and that, they enjoy their life, they learn a lot. They live to be about seventy-eight by that point.

Ricky: So specific.

Karl: I think by seventy-eight I reckon you've sort of got to that point where you go, 'D'you know what, I've done everything I'm gonna do.' If you haven't bungy jumped by the time you're seventy-eight you're not gonna do it.

Ricky: No, your hips come off.

Karl: You've done it all now. So I've had my innings, I live to be seventy-eight, but then, just as you die, you have a little baby inside you and, as you die, your life carries on.

Steve: How is this happening?

Ricky: Sorry – are you mental? I have never heard such drivel.

Karl: You're saying that but if Newton said it you'd go, 'Hmm, interesting.' That's what annoys me.

Steve: Karl, he never would. He would never say it and that's the point.

Ricky: I don't understand what you're talking about. How is there a little baby in a seventy-eight-year-old?

Karl: No, what I'm saying is – it's like an apple, where the apple grows and it's got its little baby pips in it and the apple goes and the seeds are planted and a new one's born.

Ricky: But that's what happens now.

Steve: That's what reproduction is.

Karl: But with my way, babies aren't being born left, right and centre. It's controlled so that as someone dies, someone's born.

Steve: But Karl. Stop. Whose responsibility is this?

Karl: Look, if you don't wanna do it, we won't do it!

Steve: Has Nature got to develop humans so that we live that way or is this a scientific experiment?

Ricky: What I like is, he said to you then, 'Look if you don't want to do it, we don't need to do it.' As though, if you were up for it, we'll sort it out.

Steve: We'll have a whip round and do the research.

Karl: I just think at the end of the day we've got to do something. Is anyone keeping an eye on this and looking at what we can do next to control the population thing? It does my head in that I've got to live in London for work and there's loads of people here and you know, forget going out on a Saturday night – it's too busy.

Steve: So your solution is that seventy-eight-year-old women have little babies inside them and as they slip away into death, the little babies are born?

Ricky: And who looks after the baby, because it is a pretty good system having a baby while you are young enough to look after that baby and make sure it lives to reproductive age itself.

Steve: I mean that system has been working for years. But wait a minute Nature, put that on hold, 'cos Karl Pilkington's got an idea.

Karl: That's what it was. Just an idea.

Steve: Yeah, it was nonsense, but thank you for it.

Ricky: It was the ramblings of someone you'd find by themselves, in a hospital, eating flies.

Steve: Yeah, this is the sort of thing you'd find in the diary of a psychopath who went on a rampage and then turned the gun on themselves. They'd go through his possessions and find he's drawn weird drawings, women with knives in their face, and written this kind of gobbledegook.

Ricky: I saw a similar sort of theory written out on a wall, but it was written in shit.

Karl: No, all I'm saying is, when people die normally,
          everyone's fed up about it, aren't they, and a bit
          down, but if when you pass away, you go, 'Oh
          we're going to miss Gladys' or whatever, but then
          there's this new life brought in. It's almost like a bad
          news/good news.

Ricky: But you're talking about it like someone could pick
          this idea up and run with it; like you've given them
          enough information to do it. How is this possible?
          Where does she get the baby from? How does it
          grow? Why grow it in Gladys's belly? Why not have
          it in a drawer? Just add water.

Steve: Who looks after 'Son of Gladys'?

Ricky: There is no theory here. It's the ramblings of a
          madman.

Karl: What I'm saying is the body is always changing innit
          – from caveman to now, or whatever, and they're
          always finding out more and more. Like d'you know
          how they say people have six senses?

Ricky: Yes.

Karl: Well there's loads more than that.

Ricky and Steve laugh.

Ricky: Okay, show me that you've got just one.

Karl: No, right, there's this one that's knocking about and
          what it is – say if I'm in a pub, right, and I'm just
          doing a crossword or whatever ...

Steve: ... Unlikely, but go on ...

Karl: And there's some woman who's walked in, right, and
          she's staring at me. I know she's looking at me and
          I look up and she's looking at me. They're saying
          that's a new sense that they've found out from doing
          tests and what have you.

Ricky: Yeah, it's rubbish.

Karl: And they are saying that's been around since like
          man and dinosaurs was knocking about.

Ricky: But it could be peripheral vision.

Karl: No they've explained it.

Steve: I think it's safe to assume that, with your perfectly
          round head, people are always stopping and looking
          at you.

Karl: No, but they explained it. They said it's from the
          time when caveman was wandering about and he
          would go, 'Hang on a minute' and he would look
          round and there's a dinosaur there or whatever, and
          he'd leg it.

Ricky: Right, this is nonsense. 'When caveman was
          wandering round'. Cavemen and dinosaurs, oh they
          used to live together, yeah sure. Oh that's the same
          era. What have you been watching, Raquel Welch in
          One Million Years BC?

Karl: What d'you mean?

Ricky: What do you mean, 'caveman wandering about, knocking around with a dinosaur?'

Steve: You do know *The Flintstones* is only partly based on fact?

Ricky laughs.

Steve: Dinosaurs and man did not co-exist. Dinosaurs had long gone before man arrived. Extinct, kaput.

Karl: Hmm.

Steve: What, you don't believe us because you saw that film where they took pictures of lizards and magnified them and put them next to men so they looked like they were fighting each other?

Karl: No but why couldn't that have happened? Why wasn't there dinosaurs back then? Just like we have dogs now.

Ricky: He has been watching *The Flintstones*. You know cavemen didn't mix concrete in a pelican?

Karl: I just think that there must have been a crossover point.

Ricky   Why do you think there must have been a crossover point?

Karl: Because if nothing was knocking about at any point, how did anything carry on?

Ricky: I know, exactly. Why didn't Hitler meet Nero? It's weird, there must have been a crossover, they must have met at a party somewhere. I mean are you telling me that Ken Dodd has never met Genghis Khan? They must have bumped into each other, I can't believe it!

Karl: Oh forget it.

LAZY INVENTIONS

IT ANNOYS ME HOW PEOPLE GO ON SAYING THAT PEOPLE ARE GOOD COS THEY INVENT STUFF, WHEN A LOT OF THE TIME STUFF IS INVENTED BY MISTAKE. NEWTON GOT LOADS OF PRAISE FOR COMING UP WITH GRAVITY WHEN ALL HE WAS DOING WAS CHILLIN OUT UNDER A TREE. LOADS OF OTHER PEOPLE COULD OF COME UP WITH IT BUT WERE TOO BUSY WORKIN IN A FACTORY TO BE WORRYING ABOUT FRUIT FALLING OFF A TREE. IT ALSO ANNOYS ME COS GRAVITY WASN'T CAUSING ANY PROBLEMS SO THERE WAS NO REASON TO WORRY ABOUT IT, IF WE WERE FLOATIN ABOUT BUMPIN INTO STUFF I'D SAY NEWTON SORT IT OUT BUT WE'RE NOT SO LEAVE IT.

PENICILLIN. ANOTHER EXAMPLE OF A LAZY INVENTION. IT WAS INVENTED BY A BLOKE WHO DIDNT WASH UP AFTER HIMSELF IN A SCIENCE LAB. HE WAS MIXIN SOME STUFF UP TRYING TO SORT SOMETHING OUT, ENDED UP GOING HOME WITHOUT WASHING UP HIS PLATES. HE CAME IN THE NEXT DAY TO SEE PLATES OF PENICILLIN EVERYWHERE THAT HAD GROWN THROUGH THE NIGHT.

THE ICE LOLLY WAS INVENTED BY SOME FELLA WHO WAS RELAXIN IN THE GARDEN HAVING SOME ORANGE THAT YOU ADD WATER TO, HE WENT IN WHEN IT GOT COLD. HE DIDNT TAKE HIS GLASS IN WITH HIM COS HE WAS LAZY AND THOUGHT SOMEONE ELSE CAN DO THAT FOR HIM, IT WAS A COLD NIGHT, HE GOT UP IN THE MORNING, IT HAD FROZE OVER.... THE ICE LOLLY WAS BORN.

YOGURT. SAME SORT OF STORY AS THE ICE LOLLY, SOMEONE POPPED SOME MILK IN A FRIDGE, LEFT IT IN THERE, FORGOT ABOUT IT... FANCIED A CUP OF TEA A FEW WEEKS LATER, POURED THE MILK IN AND THOUGHT 'WHATS HAPPENEND ERE', TASTED IT AND THEN THOUGHT 'I CAN SELL THIS'. THIS SORT OF DISCOVERY WILL HAPPENS LESS NOW COS OF 'USE BY' DATES.

'D'you know what, I'm sure summit's died in here.'

Karl: D'you know how you don't believe in scary stuff,
         like ghosts?

Ricky: I believe in scary stuff. I don't believe in anything
         totally illogical.

Karl: Vampires?

Ricky: No. Anything made up by man.

Karl: Well there was summit in the paper the other day
         about a vampire, how they found one. They dug
         summit up, found a body in a coffin with a bit of
         wood through its heart and a knife in its mouth.

Ricky: It was a vampire pirate?

Steve: That's definitely proof of a vampire, of course, and
         not just some grotesque murder. That's definitely
         proof of a vampire. As far as I'm aware when you've
         put the stake through the heart they just turn into
         dust.

Ricky: And all their victims get their lives back.

Karl: Right and there was a second bit. Somebody had dug it up, got the heart, blended it, burnt it, popped it in some water, drank it and they're in prison now. Now if it wasn't dodgy stuff why are they in prison?

Ricky: Because they're mental. Because they dug up a body, liquidised its heart, burnt it and drank it.

Both: That's why they're in prison!

Karl: But anyway I met Derek Acorah the other week, right.

Steve: Is he a medium that can contact the dead? Is that right?

Karl: Yeah, he just chats to 'em and that. Passes messages on.

Steve: Nice of him.

Karl: So I said, 'Tell us summit a bit weird and that.' So he said, 'What do you want to know?' and I said, 'Just summit weird.' So he goes, 'Alright then, here's one for you. There's this pub out in the country and there's this mug.' You know them old mugs that they have, where they used to leave their own cup knocking about, a tankard thing. So there was one of them mugs in there right, and everybody ...

Steve: Tankard, let's call it a tankard.

Karl: Tankard, yeah.

Ricky: 'Cos you're the only mug in this story.

Karl: So this tankard's knocking about, right, and everyone who's running the pub keeps going, 'Oh I wish they'd stop leaving this tankard about' right and they pick it up ...

Steve: It must be a pain, having a small tankard in a pub – that must be a real grind.

Karl: So they picked it up and they said, 'We'll have to wash that' and they popped it on a different sideboard. Next thing you know, that person who's touched it died.

Steve: Sure.

Karl: So they kept getting new staff and they thought 'What's the connection here?', right.

Steve and Ricky laugh.

Karl: So someone notices, and they go, 'Yeah, it's a bit weird. It's that cup, right.'

Steve: Tankard.

Karl: 'It's that tankard' and that. So they get a vicar in and they go, 'Look, there's a lot of weird stuff going on here. This tankard – every time someone touches it, they die.' So he said, 'Leave it with me.' He gets his special water out, he comes round, does a little prayer, sprinkles it. He goes, 'Right, not a problem, don't worry about it.' And he picks it up and chucks it in the bin. Guess what ...

Ricky: What?

Karl: He dies in a crash on the way home. Because he picked it up.

Ricky: But Karl, you're telling me this like it's fact.

Karl: Derek Acorah, he told me.

Ricky: But Karl, I have no opinion of that story, other than I am pretty sure there was absolutely no connection between touching the tankard and him dying. That's all I am sure of. I'm not gonna even contest the chain of events. All I'm saying is: there is no connection possible because I believe in logic and the laws of the universe. So when you're telling me about miracles and strange things you may as well be telling me about the tooth fairy and the Easter bunny. It's absolutely ludicrous.

Karl: So what would it take, though, for you to go, 'Oh I'm actually a believer now?'

Ricky: I can't answer that question because I would have to base my beliefs on some of your premises, which I can't do. It's like you saying, 'But what if you found out that two and two equalled five?' I can't. It's a necessary truth. I would have to go back and fundamentally disagree with what I think 'two-ism' and 'five-ness' is.

Karl: You've never been in a situation where you've gone, 'This room feels a bit weird?' I mean like if you've been to Cornwall on holiday, and stayed somewhere and you've gone, 'D'you know what, I'm sure summit's died in here.'

Ricky: I'm sure something has died everywhere.

Karl: I've got a mate, right, who is staying in this big
          stately home, right, and I mean it's bigger than
          Buckingham Palace this place, right. I went down
          there and from outside you go 'Oh this is brilliant'.
          It's like summit out of *To the Manor Born*. But then
          when you get in, it's a wreck. No one's doing any
          vaccing-up or anything, and there's like rat poison
          everywhere, windows are smashed. Doors kicked
          in. I think they're going to have it done up, but it's
          going to cost like £80 million. I have got a little
          torch and we're wandering around looking in all
          these different rooms, right, and I'm asking him
          'How's it got in this state?' And he was saying how
          it was a mental home at one point. And a place for
          drug addicts. Have you ever been in a hospital when
          it's been shut down or a school when there's no
          kids in it and it's got that sort of bad atmosphere of
          weirdness?

Steve: Yes, for the sake of argument.

Karl: So we're wandering about and I say, 'What's in
          this room?' And we go in and all the floors are a
          wreck and rotten and stuff. And I looked at the wall
          and there was a little piece of paper stuck on the
          wall right, and I said, 'What's this here?' And so I
          wandered over, right, got right up close to it and
          someone had wroted ...

Steve: Somebody had 'wroted'?

Karl: So there is a little sign there and it says 'Flies', with
          an arrow. I thought, 'That's a bit weird.' So I follow
          the arrow, which goes to this corner, where there's a
          shelf with about three thousand dead flies on it. And
          a condom stuck on the top! That's weird innit?

Ricky: That is weird.

Karl: Then I see there's loads of bits of paper on the floor. I picked up this bit of paper right, and it had written on it, 'Need nappies, dummy, blankets' – and I turned it over, right, and it said, 'None of this now needed – baby dead'. Now that's weird innit? That's what I'm talking about when you get a bad vibe.

Steve: I don't actually understand what point you're trying to make, Karl. Didn't you just tell us that it was once occupied by 'drug addicts and mentals', so haven't you put two and two together and thought that was probably who wrote it? That doesn't mean it's paranormal. You walk into a building, it's a big, terrifying empty house. It's terrifying in as much as it's cold, and dark and draughty. It doesn't mean that you've got some paranormal sense. 'I'm Karl Pilkington and just like Derek Acorah, I have sensed something strange and evil in this room. Wait a minute, there's some flies and a condom. I was right all along.'

Ricky: Flies and a condom was weird, but the note ... I just think of his face when he saw that. By torchlight ... You must have been terrified.

Karl: It's a bit odd, innit?

THE SCARIEST STORY EVER TOLD

I REMEMBER THIS BEING ON THE TELLY WHEN I WAS A KID. ITS A STORY ABOUT SOME WOMAN WHO WAS IN PRISON FOR DOING SOMETHING BAD. SHE WAS GONNA BE IN THERE FOR THE REST OF HER LIFE, SO SHE CAME UP WITH A PLAN TO GET HER OUT.

SHE GOT FRIENDLY WITH THE PRISON UNDERTAKER COS HE HAD THE GOODS TO HELP HER ESCAPE.

THE PLAN WAS THAT SHE WOULD GET IN A COFFIN AND HE WOULD TAKE IT TO WHERE THEY BURY THEM AND SHE WOULD GET OUT AND RUN OFF. I CANT REMEMBER WHAT HE GOT FOR HIS TROUBLE.

ANYWAY, SHE WAS IN THE COFFIN AND HE TRIED TO SHIFT IT ON HIS OWN AND ENDED UP HAVING A HEART ATTACK AND DIED.

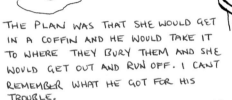

THE WOMAN DIDNT KNOW THIS HAD HAPPENED. SHE STAYED IN THE COFFIN PROBABLY THINKIN ABOUT ALL THE GOOD STUFF SHE CAN DO WHEN SHE IS FREE. SHE WAS SO RELAXED, SHE NODDED OFF AND THE NEW UNDERTAKER CHECKED HER OUT AND THOUGHT SHE WAS DEAD.

AND SO... SHE WAS BURIED ALIVE

PRISON UNDERTAKER
DIED HARD AT WORK YESTERDAY

WOMAN PRISONER WHO WILL DIE TOMMORROW

'I don't know the detail on that bit but ...'

Karl: This is one of the first Monkey News that I did and I think it's worth hearing again, just in case you forgot about it, 'cos it's sort of classic Monkey News. It's about this monkey that was knocking about called Ollie. It was called Oliver, and it was in this zoo, and it was the only monkey in there, right.

Ricky: Oh, this is the one they think was the missing link. They thought it was half human, half ape because it had a bald head and looked like you, which doesn't mean it's half anything.

Karl: What happened is, it was in the zoo and stuff and it was getting a bit lonely 'cos it was sharing its time with an elephant and a giraffe and they didn't really get on that well.

Ricky: No, no, no, no, no. Wait. They do not put chimpanzees in with the other animals.

Karl: But let me tell you ...

Ricky: Well it's not true.

Steve: Gervais, it was obviously some kind of flat share. They put an advert in the Students' Union. 'We've got two rooms to let ...'

Ricky: 'African mammal wanted.'

Karl: What I'm saying is, there was other elephants for elephants to knock about with and that. The monkey, it was the only one there. So what happened is, the zookeeper felt a bit sorry for him. He was like, 'Oh look, he's looking all fed up and that.' And like you say, I think he went a bit bald because he was bored and all that. So the zookeeper started to get pally with him and so at lunch time, when the zookeeper was sat on the wall having his ham butties or whatever, he would sort of go, 'You alright, yeah?' And Ollie used to come over, closer and closer, right. Anyway, within a month, he was sat on the wall having his lunch with him, right.

Ricky: What wall?

Karl: Just a little wall in the zoo.

Ricky: So he let the monkey out? The monkey could just wander about? He had his own door key?

Steve: These blinking latch-key monkeys.

Karl: You're picking up on little things that aren't important. It doesn't matter. So anyway, zookeeper's sat there, and as time goes on he's sort of sat with him most of the day. Monkey's walking round with him, helping him feed the other animals and that.

Ricky: This is rubbish.

Karl: But then what happened is the zookeeper, at the end of the night when he's locking up and stuff, he'd feel bad because he'd be leaving the zoo and Ollie's sat there and he's like, 'I'll see you tomorrow' and the monkey's like, 'Yeah, alright, see you later.' Ollie is looking all fed up because the zoo keeper has got a home to go to and Ollie's still stuck in his – well, where he is basically working every day. He's never going home, right. So anyway the zookeeper goes home, says to his wife, 'Look Ollie's having a bit of a time at the moment.' She says, 'Oh yeah, what's going on?' He said, 'Well he's looking a bit fed up. You know, he's sick of it.' She said, 'Bring him home.' He said, 'Well I did want to ask, but I didn't want to force it ...'

Ricky: This conversation didn't happen.

Karl: So anyway ...

Steve: Such detail!

Ricky: No it didn't happen. This is in your head.

Karl: So anyway, she said, 'Yeah, bring it home tonight.'
          So anyway, the zookeeper is looking forward to
          going into work and that. He sees Ollie. He doesn't
          tell him straightaway.

Ricky: Like it's a surprise. Oh God!

Karl: So they go through the day, you know usual stuff,
          feeding the elephants and all that. It gets to the end
          of the day and Ollie's there. He's looking at the
          zookeeper as if to say, 'Well there you go, another
          busy day over, see you tomorrow and stuff ...'

Steve: Sure. Little does he know ...

Karl: Anyway the zookeeper is like, 'Get your coat ...'

Ricky: Coat? What do you mean, 'Get your coat?'

Karl: Whatever the equivalent is, whatever you say to a
          monkey. It was kind of like, 'You're coming with
          me.' So Ollie's going 'Oh brilliant.'

Ricky: No he's not.

Steve: So Ollie gets his hat and coat ...

Karl: He can't believe his luck right. He goes back to the zookeeper's house. Everything's going well for about a week and a half, right.

Steve: Has he got his own room?

Karl: He still goes to work and stuff ...

Steve: To the zoo, yeah.

Karl: To the zoo.

Ricky: He doesn't work there!

Karl: And then he comes back with the zookeeper at night. Anyway, what ended up happening is ... he's back at the house and it's going well for about a week and a half, he's sat there, you know he's having a brandy at night before he goes to bed. The zookeeper noticed that when he took it back to work it was kind of getting flashbacks of not having a good time in the zoo, right. So, it was like, 'this isn't helping him out. He's happy when he's at home with the brandy and the fags and that, but when he comes back here, he's starting to look a bit fed up.' So he said to his wife, 'Look, you're at home all day right. I'm going to work. I'll leave him with you.' So Ollie stays at home. Anyway as time goes on there's a little bit of trouble. Whilst the fella's busy at work, grafting, paying the bills for Ollie at home, Ollie starts getting a little bit cheeky – tries it on with the missus.

Steve: Whoa! How does a monkey 'try it on with the missus'?

Karl: This is classic Monkey News.

Steve: How does he try it on?

Ricky: He's a bit drunk. He stinks of smoke. He tries it on
          with the missus. How does he try it on with her?

Karl: I don't know all the details.

Ricky: You don't know any of the details.

Karl: I don't know the detail on that bit but ...

Ricky: You don't know any of the details.

Steve: So what happens? While the zookeeper's away
          the monkey did play. What happened? Did the
          zookeeper's wife reciprocate these affections?

Karl: She probably went along with it at first. You know,
          she's cooking at home, getting the tea ready, it's
          walking past pinching her arse or whatever. And
          you know, it starts off just like it does with humans.
          It starts off as a bit of fun, before you know it ...
          Anyway, the zookeeper and his wife split up in the
          end. I think the monkey stayed with the woman.

Ricky: Honestly, your imagination.

Karl: Just put in 'monkey/chimp/Ollie' into the Internet
          and it's all there ...

'She was sort of mental homeless'

Karl: I give to charity but I feel like I'm being cheated a bit.

Ricky: You were conned by a charity weren't you?

Karl: I got stopped and they drag you in by saying, 'Have you got a gran?', and I said, 'No they died and that.' It's, 'Oh did they die of the cold?' 'No. Ill.' 'What did they have?' 'Just old age.' They said, 'Well, what happens with a lot of people's grans is they die in the cold, right.' So, I says 'That's bad innit.' So she's chatting and she's showing me pictures of these old women, who look cold, saying 'Look at her. That's Edna. She's got no family. She can't pay the bills and all that.'

Ricky: Sure.

Karl: Anyway it goes on for about fifteen minutes and you feel bad. You give 'em your bank details, right, and what happens is, every couple of months you get a letter from Edna. Well it's not from her, it's typed up and what have you, but there's a picture of Edna and it's saying 'Oh, this December Edna is going to be extra cold. It's cold outside, she can't afford to pay the heating' and what have you. So you keep paying every month like £5 or whatever. I get another letter a few months later, right, Edna's sat there – she's got a tan!

THANKS TO YOU
EDNA IS WARM
THIS WINTER

Steve: What do you mean, 'she's got a tan'?

Karl: When they said she needs money because she's cold I thought they meant for the heating – not to send her on holiday for a month. She's sat there with a tan. I'm not joking.

Steve: Are you sure it wasn't just a problem in the printing process?

Karl: No, no definitely.

Ricky: Are you sure it wasn't liver failure?

Steve: This is a terrible thing to say, but when I see those people approaching now, with the clip-boards, I always get my mobile phone out and pretend I am having a conversation.

Karl: Yeah, I've done that one.

Steve: The number of fake conversations I've had walking past them now.

Karl: I'll tell you what, we've talked about homeless people before and that, and I walked past one the other day. Don't you think that if you had a company, it's worth taking them on? Because they never have a lie in.

Ricky: Brilliant.

Karl: When does it become, like, bad to avoid homeless people? Because some people say you shouldn't, that they're people like us who have just had a bit of bad luck.

Ricky: Well of course they are.

Karl: Yeah, I know but I remember one on our estate and she was a bit – what's the word that you can use, because I don't want to offend anyone? She was sort of mental homeless. Is that a term?

Ricky: That is the official term.

Karl: Well she lived on the estate and what have you ...

Ricky: How was she homeless if she lived on the estate?

Karl: Well, she sort of decided to stay round there, because I think people on the estate spoke to her more than people who had money.

Ricky: Really?

Karl: So anyway. This mental homeless woman on the estate, what she used to do, right, she acted quite normal and she used to always push a pram around with her, right. And she was dead happy; every day she was walking up and down the road. Anyway one day she walked past me, right, and I turned round and looked in the pram – and there's a bucket with a face on it!

'I could eat a knob at night.'

Ricky: Jilly Goolden – now she ...

Steve: What's she been up to?

Ricky: Well you saw her in *I'm a Celebrity, Get Me Out of Here*?

Steve: I haven't been watching it.

Ricky: She popped a little kangaroo knob in her mouth, chewed it up.

Steve: What, it was just lying around?

Ricky: No, it was just one of the things she had to eat. Carol Thatcher, the daughter of one of our leaders, she popped a couple of bollocks in her mouth, chewed them up, swallowed them – and Jilly Goolden had to eat a dried kangaroo penis. It was so tough she couldn't even get through it.

Steve: What, it was like a Peperami?

Ricky: Yes. What do you think of that Karl?

Karl: What, eating that sort of stuff?

Ricky: Yeah.

Karl: I mean I watch it, I like those little trial bits, right, but what I don't think people realise is, right, it is hard eating a little kangaroo knob.

Steve: Really, how do you know?

Karl: No, it's just, you think about it and you go, 'Oh I couldn't do that,' but what they never mention on the TV programme – which I think takes it to the next level, right – is that they're eating that stuff at, like, half past seven in the morning – which is worse, innit? If I was there and Ant and Dec said, 'Right Karl, eat the knob' I'd go, 'Hang on a minute. Give us a few hours. Let me get some rice and that in me belly and just sort of fill myself up a little bit more. I'll pop back at about half six this evening – have it ready.' And I'd be happier then.

Steve: You don't want to eat animals' private parts on an empty stomach?

Ricky: So what are you saying?

Karl: I'm saying I could eat a knob at night.

Ricky: Just cut that there. We'll loop that. If any DJs are listening, just take that quote 'I could eat a knob at night' by Karl Pilkington and maybe do a dance remix.

Steve: Yes, maybe you are a house music producer and you could maybe get some high energy beat going and then we could send that out to some of the gay clubs. I'm sure it would be really popular.

Karl: No, but d'you know what I mean though?

Ricky: I could not do it. I couldn't pop a kangaroo testicle in my mouth and chew it. It was disgusting to watch. Good on them because they were doing it but then again I think, 'Well, they wanted to go in there.' On the one hand I think, 'Is that admirable? Is that showing good British mettle or is it "I'll do anything to get on telly for a week?"' Where does it stop? I thought Rebecca Loos went too far when she gave the little pig a tug, but at least she knew where to stop.

Steve: I think it's obvious when you have to stop – the pig tells you that.

Ricky: Where is there a kangaroo hopping around without a cock?

Karl: Here's another question right – a bit of a spin off with animals and that. Have you ever, Steve, killed a fly?

Steve: Probably, yes.

Karl: Right. Well I was watching David Attenborough, right. He makes his money out of flies and that, don't he. D'you think he's ever killed one, or does he go, 'Well I can't kill that fly or that spider 'cos that's how I make my money'?

Ricky: I don't know what the question is.

Karl: Right, me mam, right, she said, if a fly is knocking about the house, she never kills it. She always catches it and puts it out and that. She said she'd never kill one.

Ricky: Who is she, Mr Miyagi? What do you mean, 'she catches it'? How does she catch it?

Steve: With a pair of chopsticks.

'Let me just tell you the ending ...'

Karl: D'you know the other week when I came up with a different idea of how we can make the world run and that.

Steve: Can we just have a quick recap of that because I seem to remember it was a load of old arse.

Ricky: It was ridiculous. It was saying that the world is over-populated so we should have a system whereby people live until they are seventy-eight – I don't know how you can enforce that – but when they die they've got a little baby in their stomach, like a pip in an apple, and the baby carries on when they die. It wasn't a theory, it was the ramblings of a mental case.

Karl: Anyway listen, right, I've been thinking about it, right, and if we can't do that, right, if it's a 'no' to that idea ...

Ricky: It is a 'no'.

Karl: ... Here's another idea ...

Ricky: Ooh, you could win the Nobel prize for this one ...

Karl: There is a lot of ways in't there, in the world, that some creatures and that go about sort of moving on, if you know what I mean ...

Ricky: Not really. Do you mean evolution?

Karl: Yes, on that David Attenborough programme he's always showing, yeah, little insects and what they have got to do. And there was one about a wasp, right, that had to fly about, right, for ages, looking out for a certain type of spider, right.

Ricky: Which it lays its eggs in, correct.

Karl: It whizzes down, it lands on its back, so it's got to get that right. I don't think the spider's up for anything, the spider isn't even aware of this. It's not going, 'I've got to look out for a wasp', even though all this has got to be perfect timing. So this wasp dived down right, sat on the back of this spider, it injects it or something, with a maggot or something, right – and then that maggot lives off the spider for a bit. The spider knows it's got a maggot in it.

Ricky: No it doesn't.

Karl: It does.

Ricky: No it doesn't.

Karl: And it's making a web for it. It goes, 'I've got something to look after here now. I've got responsibilities.' It makes a web, right. It sort of reverses into it and puts the maggot on the web. The maggot sort of clings on to the web, maggot eats the spider – and then it moves on. Now if I came up with that idea you'd say, 'That's never gonna happen.'

Ricky: Wake up! It's not the fact that you came up with the idea for an old lady dying at seventy-eight with a baby growing in her – even though it's nonsense, it's no idea – it's how could it be enforced. Even if scientists thought that was the best idea in the world how would they make it happen? Who's gonna go, 'That's a good idea, we've never thought of that, get in Elsie. Elsie, we wanna try something ...'

Karl: Who told the wasp to look out for that spider? To go on its back?

Ricky: What do you mean 'Who told the wasp?' – It's evolution, it's natural selection ...

Karl: Yeah but say, like, we have a kid at the moment. You don't just jump on the back of a woman and go 'There you go love' and then a baby pops out.

Steve: You do if you come from Bristol.

Karl: No what I'm saying is, right, you build up to it don't you. You have a bit of a chat and you go, 'How's it going?', 'Alright yeah,' and you get on and that – and then a little baby will come out.

Steve: Oh, that's how babies are made is it? You have a chat, and you go 'alright' and a little baby comes out.

Ricky: That is amazing.

Steve: Man alive – this is incredible.

Karl: What I'm saying is at what point is a wasp ever gonna have a chat with a spider or meet up with it?

Steve: I don't even understand where we are now in this conversation.

Ricky: 'At what point is a wasp gonna ever have a chat with a spider?' What world do you live in? What's in your head? I can't believe it. 'At what point is a wasp ever gonna have a chat with a spider ...?'

Steve: So in some kind of weird insect nightclub these wasps and these maggots are meeting and getting on. Is that how you imagine it?

Karl: No, but that's what I'm saying to you. What are the odds on that actually happening?

Ricky: Listen – behaviour in lower forms of life is purely chemical. It bypasses any form of consciousness. There is a parasite that lays its egg in a stickleback, okay, and it literally has to change the stickleback's behaviour because it has to get into a warm-blooded animal to complete its cycle. So what it does is – this parasite makes the stickleback not flee from the shadow of a heron – it makes the stickleback get eaten! So it then is in the belly of a warm-blooded animal and it can complete its life cycle. But at no point is this parasite going, 'Slow down, there's a heron coming. Stay here. Stay here.' And the stickleback isn't going, 'Why? I don't wanna stay here, there's a heron.' There's no conversation. It's not like they get together and go, 'Listen I have got something that might be mutually beneficial to both of us. I need to get into a heron.' 'Hey, you like to be eaten by a heron but I don't ...'

Karl: No, all I'm saying is you know the idea that I came up with – well, you're saying that's crazy.

Steve: How many times have we heard 'All I am saying is' and then such a stream of nonsense that it's blown our minds?

Karl: No, but that's all I'm saying – what you've just explained there with the heron having to knock about and for a flea to be sat in the shade and that ...

Ricky: Now that is incredible. That's his translation of what I just said. That sums it up for me. He sees a headline, he reads a book, it then goes through this weird filtering system. And I imagine there is music in his head – it's 'boo bi boom ba eh oh bi ba' – like a discordant piano.

Steve: I think the noise in Karl's head is like a fax machine at full volume. Errrrrrrrrrr!

Ricky: I think it's like music from a Czechoslovakian cartoon from 1963. Odd noises, woks being banged, pianos being hit by elbows.

Steve: He is the only person you can give a body of information to and he strips away the facts.

Ricky: The way he said that. I clearly talked about some sort of parasite in a stickleback that makes its behaviour change so it doesn't flee the heron's shadow. He said, 'So there's an 'eron with a flea who doesn't like the shade.' How did it get to that?

Karl: It doesn't matter – forget that right – but anyway ...

Ricky: What's your theory?

Karl: What I'm saying is, I've come up with summit else that I wanna run by you then.

Ricky: Go on then.

Karl: As you have sort of boo boo'd the other idea ...

Ricky: Boo boo'd?

Steve: We have boo boo'd it.

Ricky: He's chosen a completely different bear. It was originally 'Pooh Pooh the Bear' but now it's 'Boo Boo the Bear'. Brilliant!

Karl: ... You've said no to the old woman having a kid before she dies. What about if we do it the other way, right? Somehow, I don't know how yet ...

Ricky: A kid has an old lady?

Steve: That's what it's going to be isn't it? A child gives birth to an old man.

Karl: No, what I'm saying is, right, work the other way round ...

Rick: Come on then.

Karl: So if somehow we can inject something into a body that's just died, right ...

Rick: Listen to this. Imagine his notes. When he hands them into the Nobel people and they say 'If there's a way that we can inject something'. And the Nobel committee go 'Well what?' 'Well I don't know the chemical formula but something. Something HO_2...'

Karl: So anyway, you inject it in the temple.

Steve: He's narrowed it down to 'the temple'.

Karl: So you inject it in.

Rick: Who are you injecting?

Karl: This old woman who's been ill and that and she's died.

Steve: So she's dead? We're bringing old people back to life? Okay, fine, we've just got to sort that out first, but fine, we'll crack that, so go on – next.

Karl: This is a way of controlling population remember. They can't be having it away and having kids. This is just the way we've got to work now.

Ricky: Okay, so there is an old lady. What happens?

Karl: Right. So you get, like, an old woman ...

Steve: ... Who is dead ...

Karl: Right, inject her and that ...

Steve: Inject her!

Karl: ... And then what happens is – she sort of wakes up, right, and she works the other way. So she might be seventy-seven and then she'll have a birthday and she's seventy-six and she's working that way, if you know what I mean. Okay, are you with me ...?

Ricky: I'm really scared. This is the maddest thing you've ever said. This is madder than the old lady with the pip like an apple in her belly.

Karl: That sort of did work.

Ricky: No it didn't work. It worked in your head. It's like you had a dream and you woke up and went, 'Oh I've got a great theory.'

Karl: Let me just tell you the ending because the ending works out a bit better. What I'm saying is when you die at the age of ...

Ricky: Seventy-eight.

Karl: Nine months.

Ricky: What?

Karl: At the age of nine months. 'Cos that's when you die.

Ricky: What do you mean when you die at the age of nine months?

Karl: You're not scared of dying because you're now a baby so you don't know what's going on anyway.

Steve: Rick, I think when she's in her twenties, she's in her old age.

Karl: Yeah but it doesn't matter because that's the fun part of your life, innit, when you're twenty and you've got all your energy and that – so before you die you're actually having a good life rather than it being the other way round.

Ricky: But does she do different stuff than she did on the way up? Because she has already lived seventy-eight years don't forget. She was already a baby once and grew up and then someone stuck a needle in her head and said, 'Right, back you go.'

Karl: No ... well forget all that bit.

Ricky: So she died and she doesn't remember her first life. This is a new life is it?

Karl: Let me just leave you with this ...

Ricky: You're talking shit – explain yourself.

Karl: What I'm saying is – old people are scared of dying. When they're seventy-seven they're going, 'Oh, what's going to happen to me?' Little injection in the head; it goes backwards; when it's a baby everybody is around it going, 'Yeah, it's gonna die soon.' But the baby hasn't got a clue, it's happy. It's playing about with its rattle or whatever, it's not scared.

Ricky: So it loses all its memories?

Karl: That's it.

AGING BACKWARDS IDEA

Ricky: And then what happens – when does it die? When it gets to nought? When it's nought days old?

Karl: Yeah, it just dies. People know, it's almost like a countdown. So the family's aware of it.

Steve: But aren't the family getting younger as well? What's happened to the family?

Karl: Forget it then. We'll leave it as it is.

Ricky: Leave it as it is, shall we?

Steve: Can we all agree on that now, guys? Shall we leave it as it is?

Ricky: You're a fucking maniac.

'And you've got the goat going "What am I doing here?"'

Ricky: Everyone have a nice Christmas? Good presents, Karl?

Karl: Yeah ... yeah.

Steve: A friend of mine gave the gift of a goat. On behalf of a charity organisation you can give someone else the gift of a goat for an African family. So you say, 'I've bought you "goat,"' and they say, 'Oh brilliant where is it?' and you go, 'No, it's going to a family in Africa.' It's a sort of good will thing.

Ricky: So you buy an African family a goat?

Steve: And it will help them for years. It's a beautiful idea. But I thought to myself straightaway – knowing Karl's views on charity and giving – what would his view be?

Karl: Are they happy with the present over there? Is the African family going, 'Oh I hope someone gets us a goat for Christmas?'

Ricky: You're an idiot. What, you think an African family wakes up and there's a little goat with a ribbon tied round it and they go, 'Oh look what Santa brought us.'

Steve: 'And that mince pie's gone and that glass of milk ...'

Ricky: You're such an idiot.

Karl: No, no, no, but what I'm saying is, does that family want a goat?

Steve: Yes.

Karl: But why?

Ricky: It's not that they *want* a goat, they *need* a goat. Are they going to say, 'Oh I wanted a Nintendo?' What are you thinking?

Karl: What I'm saying is, right, let me put myself in their shoes ...

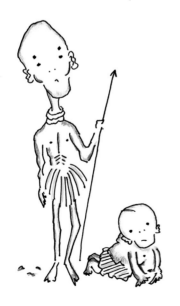

Steve: This'll be a first.

Karl: ... Well, they haven't got any shoes but say I'm one
          of them over there, right. I'm hungry, I'm sat there,
          it's Christmas Day, I open the present. Little goat
          there right. Now if I was one of them I'd be going,
          'Not another mouth to feed.' At the end of the day,
          there isn't enough food to go round for themselves,
          never mind the goat. Don't they say having a dog is
          quite expensive, what with all the injections you've
          got to give it? And the tinned food and everything,
          it mounts up. What I'm saying is, that's all very well
          giving them a goat, but who's looking after it?

Ricky: Well I'm assuming it's all above board. The goat's
          had its injection. That's what some of the money
          goes towards. It's given to the family so they can
          milk it and have milk and cheese and whatever. I
          don't think it's a burden. What do you mean, 'they
          wake up Christmas Day and open a present'?

Steve: 'There's a goat-shaped thing in wrapping paper, I
          wonder what that could be. I hope it's that goat we
          asked for ... My God, it is!'

Karl: The thing is, why do they want that goat? What's the
          main reason? What does a goat give you?

Both: Milk!

Karl: Milk, right. Now wouldn't it be easier to just send
          them a bottle of milk without all the hassle and
          headaches that come with it? That's all I'm saying.
          And the other thing is, think about the goat. That
          was happy over here. Suddenly it's on barren land,
          no grass ...

Ricky laughs.

Ricky: I'm gonna burst. What do you mean?

Steve: They didn't send a goat from *here.*

Karl: I'm saying who's happy at the end of this? You've
         got a fella over here who hasn't got a present
         because his mate bought him a goat. He's not happy.
         Then you've got the person who's opened it who
         wanted summit else. It's a goat. They go, 'Tut, who's
         going to look after this?' They're not happy. And
         you've got the goat, going 'What am I doing here ...?'

Steve and Ricky are in hysterics.

THE PROBLEM WITH CHARITY IS IT NEVER ENDS

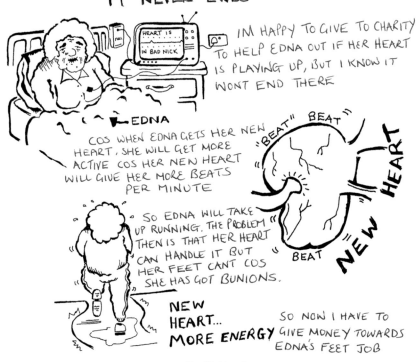

IM HAPPY TO GIVE TO CHARITY TO HELP EDNA OUT IF HER HEART IS PLAYING UP, BUT I KNOW IT WONT END THERE

HEART IS IN BAD NICK

EDNA

COS WHEN EDNA GETS HER NEW HEART, SHE WILL GET MORE ACTIVE COS HER NEW HEART WILL GIVE HER MORE BEATS PER MINUTE

"BEAT" BEAT "

"NEW HEART"

BEAT

SO EDNA WILL TAKE UP RUNNING. THE PROBLEM THEN IS THAT HER HEART CAN HANDLE IT BUT HER FEET CANT COS SHE HAS GOT BUNIONS.

NEW HEART... MORE ENERGY

SO NOW I HAVE TO GIVE MONEY TOWARDS EDNA'S FEET JOB

THEN.. WHEN SHE COMES OUT OF HOSPITAL, HER FEET ARE A BIT SMALLER COS THEY HAVE CHIPPED THE BONE AWAY, SO NOW SHE'S ASKIN FOR MORE MONEY FOR A NEW PAIR OF TRAINERS

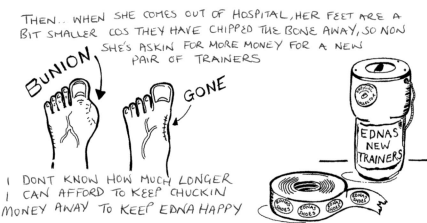

BUNION

GONE

EDNAS NEW TRAINERS

EDNAS SHOES

I DONT KNOW HOW MUCH LONGER I CAN AFFORD TO KEEP CHUCKIN MONEY AWAY TO KEEP EDNA HAPPY

'Err ...'

Steve: Karl, if you could have a superpower, like Superman, what would your superpower be?

Ricky: Can I suggest consciousness? The power of thought?

Steve: Remember you have already got opposable thumbs. Cross that one off the list. But there are so many others to choose from: telepathy, x-ray vision ...

Ricky: ... Flight, invisibility ...

Steve: Choose it wisely.

Ricky: ... Strength, intelligence ...

Karl: But why have I been picked?

Steve: Oh for God's sake.

Karl: No, no, but I'm just saying ...

Steve: It's just a question.

Karl: Does anyone else want this, because with that comes a responsibility?

Steve: With great power does come great responsibility ...

Ricky: So would you like spidey senses? Is that what you're saying?

Karl: Err ...

Ricky: Would you like some sense?

Karl: Err ...

Steve: Come on Karl! You know the sort of powers superheroes have.

Karl: I know but they're never happy are they? Spiderman wanted to tell that girl that he could climb walls and that. He's like, 'I can't'. Superman never told Lewis, and that.

Ricky: Who's Lewis?

Steve: Lewis. That was just Superman's pen pal.

Karl: You know Hulk. He wasn't happy.

Steve: But you're being allowed to choose the superpower. You don't have to get it forced upon you, like the Hulk.

Ricky: Hulk. He wasn't happy. It's true. He's got a point. There's not many happy superheroes are there?

Steve: Leaving aside the superheroes you're already aware of, what superpower would you want? You don't have to fight crime with it, Karl.

Ricky: Everyone around the world now is thinking, 'What will Karl choose?'

Steve: Let me just remind you of some of the other things available. Invisibility ...

Karl: All the time, though, or could I turn that on and off?

Steve: Let's say you could turn that on and off. Would that interest you?

Karl: Yeah. I'll have that.

Steve: Right, okay, and what would you do with this power of invisibility?

Karl: Just sort of wander about, and that, and just not get seen.

Ricky: Brilliant choice, and put to such great use. Well done.

Steve: And why would you want to wander around and not be seen? What would you gain from that?

Karl:	Errr ... You could sort of go in shops when they're shut, so you don't have to go with the crowds.
Ricky:	How would you get in?
Karl:	Just get in, just before they lock up.
Ricky:	Okay. How would you get out?
Karl:	Wait till the morning.
Ricky:	Brilliant.
Steve:	So hang on, that's your use of invisibility? You're given the power of invisibility and you want to sneak into a shop, wait for twelve hours, and then buy something?
Ricky:	Oh I love it.
Steve:	Just so that you don't have to be there with other people?
Karl:	D'you know what, I don't want it. I don't want a power.
Steve:	Why not?
Karl:	'Cos I just don't think it'll do me any good. I think it's more of a hindrance.

Steve and Ricky laugh.

'The menu is like a book now, innit?'

Steve: Karl, if you had to eat the same dinner every day for the rest of your life, what would you eat?

Karl: You see it depends, dunnit? I mean I mainly eat just so I keep going. I am not that bothered, I don't really taste it anyway. I just shove it down.

Steve: What, like a horse?

Karl: At what point did it become important that things were sort of seasoned or garnished to go with it and stuff? At the end of the day we're all eating, aren't we, so you can move about and that, and you've got energy.

Ricky: But we need to know what we're tasting don't we, because we need to have certain things. We need sugar, we need salt. So we need to know what they taste like to know we're getting them.

Karl: Now we have got chefs so leave that up to them, to make sure we are getting enough salt.

Ricky: But I thought you were talking about this from an
           evolutionary standpoint ...

Steve: Do you think that's likely?

Ricky laughs.

Karl: No, but leave it for them to make sure we are getting
           safe food. I mean to be honest, it annoys me the way
           people worry about food now and how there's so
           much to choose from. I think it's got out of hand.

Steve: Any form of choice really worries you doesn't it?
           You don't like choice.

Karl: No. Choice is good, but not too much. It's like with
           anything now. If you go into a toffee shop, there's
           loads of ...

Ricky: Sorry, where are you going to find a toffee shop?

Steve: So, you're in a fairy tale ...

Ricky: Yeah, you're in a Dickens story in the nineteenth
           century ...

Steve: You're in *Shrek* ...

Ricky: ... And you go into a toffee shop.

Steve: What's your point?

Karl: What I'm saying is you go into a shop full of toffees ...

Steve: You've just come from the candlestick maker ...

Karl: Right, you go in there and there's just too much choice. I can stand there for up to, like, four minutes sort of going ...

Steve: 'Up to four minutes'?

Ricky: So he's in a toffee shop ... in a top hat ...

Steve: But he's only got four minutes because he has to go down to the pea green boat that he's sailing off in ...

Karl: Well forget the toffee ...

Steve: So you'd prefer it was just one selection of toffee?

Karl: Well maybe two. What I'm saying is, right, there is now too much choice. Whenever you get a menu in a restaurant, it's not like you just go, 'Oh right, what is there? Yeah I'll have that.' There's too much. The menu is like a book now, innit? And you've got to that point now that people are even taking a risk when they're eating.

Ricky: What do you mean?

Karl: Erm ... you know in Japan or China or something
          they are eating that fish that if it's not cooked right,
          it can kill you. Not worth the risk, when there's so
          many other fish. Like mackerel! Or have a bit of cod
          or whatever. As soon as there's a risk, take it off the
          menu.

Ricky: Yes I totally agree.

Karl: Not worth it.

'Things like that always get me thinking ...'

Steve: Karl, you said that your New Year's resolution was that you were going to learn something every day.

Karl: Yeah, if I can.

Steve: Have you learned anything today?

Karl: Today? Well I don't know the full facts of it but ...

Ricky: Could I just say that when someone says they learn something new every day, it doesn't count if they forget it the next day. Because that'd be Groundhog Day learning.

Karl: Well the thing I learned today was about an octopus. You know they have got eight legs and that?

Ricky: Tentacles.

Karl: They can use six of them legs to cover their head, so that they look like a little stone – and use the other two to run off.

Ricky: He's thinking of Squiddly Diddly.

Steve: Yeah, he's picturing a Disney cartoon.

Karl: But anyway ...

Steve: So in your mind he's singing a song and running off ...

Karl: But anyway, something else I learned, right. It's mainly about animals and that 'cos that's normally quite interesting. There's a chicken somewhere ...

Ricky: Oh yeah, specific.

Karl: ... And the owner of it was getting fed up because he had to feed it and that but it wasn't giving anything back.

Steve: No eggs?

Karl: No eggs, right. So he was like, 'Oh I am sick of this.' Anyway, someone told him to pop a little axe next to its little house, right, so when it comes out in the morning thinking 'Oh, I'll have another lazy day doing nothing', he'd see this axe and suddenly think, 'Oh, aye.'

Steve: 'I'm for the chop', it thought?

Karl: Next day it laid about six eggs.

Ricky: It's rubbish! The chicken wouldn't recognise the axe as a threat. It wouldn't be able to reason, 'Oh I'd better start working or I'll be meat.' It's absolute rubbish. Once again it's this ridiculous thing where you personify animals and give them reasoning powers that are better than yours. I mean you make chickens and monkeys cleverer than you in your stories, which is weird. It didn't happen and wouldn't work. Next. What else haven't you learned today?

Karl: Well, as always, things like that always get me thinking ...

Steve: His mind's working now. This apparently has got his mind working.

Karl: Well d'you think, then, that it's worth looking after animals if there isn't any memory? If they don't know what's happening anyway? You're always going on about don't be cruel to things.

Ricky: Why would you be cruel? Why would you ever want to be cruel to an animal, whether it can reason or not?

Karl: No, no, I don't mean really cruel. But there's an advert that's on in Britain advertising some supermarket and it's saying, 'Before we kill our chickens, they have a great life.' They have this voice-over and you see a happy chicken, and they're going, 'We give it a good little house to live in. It's got straw. It eats good, and then we kill it.'

Ricky: Well that's better, isn't it?

Karl: I don't think it is though is it, because at the end of the day, if I was that chicken, right, I am that chicken loving me life. I can't believe me luck, right. I've got a nice little field, nice food and everything, but I'm gonna die.

Ricky: Yeah, we're all gonna die.

Karl: But then, if you were a rubbish chicken, that had a rubbish life, you'd be going, 'Oh kill me.'

Ricky: Karl, they're not thinking about what's going to happen tomorrow. A chicken's not going, 'I'm fed up with this. I can't wait for that axe to be used on my neck.'

Karl: Well now that you've mentioned the cutting off of an 'ead, right, on a chicken, that's something else I have learned right ...

Ricky: His mind is like a pin ball, isn't it? Ding, dong, bong, 'chicken', ding, dong, 'head off', bink, doink.

Karl: No, this was in a proper science magazine, so you can't have a go. This wasn't something on the internet, this was printed in a magazine.

Steve: Okay and what was it?

Ricky: Here comes the filter. It's going to come out nonsense. You could have Professor Stephen Hawking sitting there, whispering stuff in your ear, but when you said it – gobbledegook.

Karl: Well let's see then. What they've done is they've done another experiment, right. They've cut somebody's head off. And you know how they used to do it in the olden days, where they'd put your head in a stock, cut it off for whatever reason, right? You've done something wrong, right, and the question that everybody used to talk about in the village was, you know, 'Oh I made eye contact with it and it was a bit worrying because he was looking at me and he looked fed up and that.'

Ricky: Right, he's dead.

Karl: So they've put a bit of work into this and they've done it again somewhere and they have worked out that when the head comes off the body, it stays alive for thirty seconds.

Ricky: No, they don't know that. They can never know that.

Karl: No, they did this experiment ...

Ricky: No. There are loads of issues here. No one's experimenting with human beings by cutting their head off. No, no, no, no!

Steve: You read this in what? *Executioners' Monthly*?

Karl: No, but this is where it gets weird, right. So the head's off, right, and what they did was they chucked a load of questions at it.

Ricky laughs.

74

Ricky: So the head lands perfectly back on the neck and goes, 'What d'you wanna know?'

Karl: Ah, but it said ...

Ricky: So they are asking questions and it's going, 'D'you know what – to be quite honest I don't want to answer your questions. I am a little bit annoyed about the execution still.'

Karl: Well that was the interesting thing. They said ...

Ricky: No. It didn't happen, Karl. Oh, don't talk shit. What are you talking about? These people round in white coats going, 'Quick, answer the question, you're bleeding.'

Karl: Right, so they talked to it for about twenty-five to thirty seconds. The last five seconds it sort of can't be bothered answering them. But apart from that they were chucking questions at it. I don't think it spoke. I don't think it was two and two equals four and stuff. It was more to do with blinking.

Steve: So blink once for 'yes', blink twice for 'no'?

Ricky: Oh yeah, so they said to the bloke, 'Listen, when you die, you are probably not going to be able to talk because your jaw is going to be on the ground, you're not going to be able to open your mouth. If you do, you'll fall over backwards and hit your head. So instead, blink once for "yes" and twice for "no".' 'Yeah, alright, yeah. Is the axe nice and shiny?' The thing is they wouldn't be able to do it with you, Karl, because if they cut your head off, it would just roll away because it is perfectly spherical.

Steve: Plus, whenever you ask Karl anything, it takes about twenty seconds for him to process the question and start to formulate an answer.

'You mention it once, suddenly it's the talk of the town.'

Karl: We were talking about sayings and that, right. 'A stitch in time saves nine.' I'm never going to use that, I don't think. Anyway ...

Ricky: You're never going to understand it fully, are you?

Karl: Suzanne repairs me stuff anyway. It doesn't really matter. But what about the one in greenhouses and that?

Ricky: 'People who live in glass houses shouldn't throw stones.'

Karl: Yeah.

Steve: Does that confuse you? You've never understood that one?

Karl: No, that's a lot clearer innit. It's sort of saying, 'Don't be chucking stuff about if you're surrounded by glass and what have you.'

Ricky: Yeah, but don't forget – it's an analogy. It's a metaphor. It's not to be taken literally. It's not really talking to people who live in glass houses.

Steve: Sorry, before you say that, Rick, I'm intrigued to know if he's fully got to grips with this. Just give us your explanation again of what you take it to mean.

Karl: Well, just don't be chucking stuff about, really.

Ricky: If that's what it means, they would just say that.

Karl: No, no, but that saying has been around a lot longer than we think. That's when people probably did live in basic glass houses. What they mean now is ...

Ricky: No no no no, whoa whoa whoa. Sorry, so cavemen went from rock to a nice crystal structure, did they? What you talking about? When do you think we lived in glass houses?

Karl: Well, when that saying is used now they mean sort of plasma tellies. Or ornaments.

Ricky: No they don't.

Karl: They are saying, 'Don't chuck stuff about because you'll break it.'

Ricky: No, it's not about damaging your own property.

Steve: They don't mean you shouldn't throw rocks inside your own 'glass house'.

Ricky: It's a metaphor. It means, 'Don't be having a go at people if you yourself have got more to lose.' Do you know what I mean? Don't start a war if you could come off bad as well. It's about how fragile your situation is. If you live in a glass house – metaphorically – don't throw stones at someone else because when he throws stones back at you, your house is more easily damaged than his. Again, metaphorically.

Steve: It doesn't mean that if you're living in a glass house don't throw bricks about – because that would be a very specific audience that the phrase was trying to reach.

Ricky: Okay, I think we have got to the crux of this. Karl, what is an analogy?

Karl: It's sort of like a little story told quickly, innit.

Steve: 'It's a little story told quickly.' To what end?

Karl: Well it depends what the story is.

Ricky: Give me an analogy.

Karl: Well I thought of one with the greenhouse, right.

Steve: Now it's a greenhouse. Before it was just a glass house.

Karl: Alright then, a glass house.

Ricky: That glass house is metaphorical. It's about the
          fragility of your situation ...

Karl: You see I just prefer to say what you mean so here's
          mine; 'People who live in a glass house have to
          answer the door.'

Ricky: I don't know what that means. You may be a genius
          because I don't get that. 'People who live in glass
          houses have to answer the door?'

Steve: Let's hear his explanation.

Karl: Because the people knocking at the door will be able
          to see you, 'cos it's a glass house. So don't pretend
          you're not in.

Ricky: There is no analogy or metaphor for you, is there?
          You literally mean if you live in a glass house and
          someone knocks on the door you have to answer it.
          There is no hidden meaning there, is there?

Steve: You have to add a number of other caveats, surely?
          'If you live in a glass house don't walk around
          naked.'

Karl: Yeah.

Ricky: You see these are literal. You could actually make
          that into quite a nice saying. If someone said that
          to me and they weren't a shaved chimp, I would
          think that means, 'If you have chosen to be totally
          open all the time you can't go back on it. If you

wear everything on your sleeve, if you shout about
everything, you can't have any secrets because people
can see through you.'

Karl: It can mean that as well, yeah.

Steve: Oh that's handy. I love the fact that in your head
         there should be sayings for people who actually live
         in glass houses. Who is it that is living in a glass
         house?

Karl: I didn't start it. It's just if everyone else is bringing
         up about these people who are living in glass houses,
         let's get to the real problems we've got.

Ricky: 'People who live in glass houses should live near a
         glazier.'

Karl: What? Look, here's another saying, right, that
         I learnt recently from a mate, right. 'There's an
         elephant in the room.'

Ricky: Okay, I haven't heard that one but explain it to me.

Karl: It's like when you ... er ... when something's going on
         in a room, right, but no one is mentioning it because
         everyone's a bit too sort of ... but in a way it's better
         that it's out. It's like how whenever we go out for
         something to eat or a drink or something – normally
         after about five minutes, the topic gets on to the
         shape of my head.

Ricky: Yeah, yeah. Well I can't resist the shape of your
         head.

Karl: Right, so you're happy talking about it.

Ricky: It's not just the shape though, is it? It's the state of it as well. Outside and in. I mean his head is a fascinating little *objet d'art*. It's perfectly round. It's got no hair where it should have and it's hollow.

Steve: The features are slightly too small for the face.

Ricky: Unbelievable.

Karl: No, but what I'm saying is, I'm the elephant in the room, right. Nobody's talking about it. You mention it once, suddenly it's the talk of the town.

Ricky laughs.

Karl: What I mean is everybody starts joining in going, 'Well yeah, it is round, but it does suit you' and these are people who I don't even know sometimes, and they're all dipping in, and that is an 'elephant in the room'.

Steve: So you don't want people to discuss the shape of your head, or the lack of hair? You would feel happier if they didn't mention it?

Karl: Sometimes I think it is better that it's out there. It's made me a stronger person though. It's the same way we were talking about religion and that. Samson and Delilah. He got weaker without hair. Whereas with me, it's made me stronger because it's almost like it's treated like a disability. Everybody's sort of mentioning it, and talking about it. 'What's it like having a bald head?' So it has made me stronger.

Ricky: But would you ever wear a wig?

Karl: Erm ... Not really.

Ricky: A long wig so you looked like Samson.

Karl: Well the only time I wanted a wig was when I did
          jury duty once, and it was annoying that I was sat
          on the jury right in front of these criminals, right.
          Everybody else has got disguises. The judges have
          them wigs on, right.

Ricky: That's not a disguise.

Karl: That's a disguise. That's why judges wear 'em.

Ricky: No. Why print their name in the paper and have a
          picture of them? What do you mean, 'it's a disguise'?

Karl: It's a disguise, innit?

Ricky: No, if it was a disguise, they'd go in with one of
          those glasses with a nose and a beard attached. All
          judges would look like Groucho Marx if it was a
          disguise.

Karl: Well I am just saying, that's what annoyed me when
          I was sat there on the front row. I couldn't have
          been any closer to the criminals. I was sat there and
          I thought, 'Why didn't I just pop a little wig on, or a
          pair of glasses?'

Ricky laughs

Ricky: I would have loved to have seen you in the front row at Crown Court.

Steve: Except in this country you're not allowed to show pictures of jurors. You can't take photos in a courtroom. So there's always these sketch artists that draw drawings and they're on the news. The idea that we'd have seen a sketch of eleven people and a Krusty the Clown figure would have been amazing.

Ricky: Yeah, I would have loved to have seen the artist's drawing of you. Because it would have been carefully drawn people and then just a little round head.

Steve: Or Charlie Brown.

Ricky laughs.

Ricky: Yeah, Charlie Brown sitting on the end.

'What d'you mean about eyes facing forward?'

Steve: A question for Karl, 'What body parts can you live without?' Obviously someone having sleepless nights thinking about this.

Ricky: He can live without a brain.

Steve: He's coped this far.

Karl: So the bits that I've got now, if I had to get rid of one of 'em, what won't I miss?

Steve: Yes.

Karl: I did a bit of an experiment on this, right. At home, Suzanne does the cooking, it's my job to wash up.

Ricky: She gives you all the really big responsible jobs? She pays the bills and wires the house and you go, 'What can I do?' and she says, 'Well you can go and play with the worms in the garden.'

Karl: So anyway, it's my job to wash up and I thought to really make it interesting I wonder if I can do it if I didn't have any thumbs?

Ricky laughs.

Ricky: And so what did you do?

Steve: You sliced off your thumbs?

Karl: I just sort of held 'em in and it's amazing how it took
         me ages, just having that one thing gone.

Ricky: It's part of our evolution, the opposable thumb.
         Basically that's when we soared. These are
         milestones in evolution. The opposable thumb,
         the forward facing eyes, walking upright. These
         are massive things that take us out of the animal
         kingdom.

Steve: And one day, Karl, you'll walk upright.

Karl: What d'you mean about eyes facing forward? D'you
         mean before we got here there was people whose
         eyes were looking in their head?

Ricky and Steve laugh.

Karl: I don't understand.

Ricky: No, no, I'm going way back. I'm not saying chimps
         had eyes on the side of their head. I'm talking major
         milestones in any evolution. Er ... I lost you at
         evolution, I think.

Steve: So when you were doing this washing up
         experiment, you say that you found it difficult, it
         took you ages. So you didn't just give up once you
         realised how essential thumbs were? You actually
         washed up everything?

Ricky: I just think of Suzanne walking in and Karl's there, just covered in water and Fairy Liquid suds, standing on a pile of broken crockery.

Steve: Yeah, plunging his face into the sink every thirty seconds and just swishing his head around.

Karl: Well we talked about the washing up thing before. I look out of a window, because the sink is in front of the window, and that's why I quite like washing up, because I can just look out onto the street, see people going past. But I was looking across the way right, and there's some sort of Chinese people who live in a really small flat, and they're up till all hours. I don't know what they're doing, but they decide to vac up about half past three in the morning. They're always really noisy and that, but above them, there was some woman, right, whose bedroom is on par to our kitchen, right. So I'm sort of washing up, and I look across and see this woman with like, no pants on and that, no bra and that ...

Steve: 'Naked.'

Ricky: That's the word you're looking for.

Karl: Yeah, yeah, she's just wandering about with nowt on and that. So I was like, 'Oh.' So I carried on washing up and kept looking. And I was looking and she looked at me, right. So we made eye contact. So I was like, 'Oh God.' So what I thought the best thing to do was, sort of drop me pants a little bit, just a little bit. I had boxer shorts on. If I just show a little bit of arse cheek then it's kind of like we're quits, right.

Steve: I don't understand your thinking.

Karl: So Suzanne's watching the telly, right. She turned
            round to see how I'm getting on with the washing
            up and she sees me with me pants down a little bit
            with me arse out. She said, 'What you doing?' I said,
            'Don't look now, but there's a woman over the road
            with no pants on and that. She caught me looking. I
            am just giving her a bit back.'

Ricky: I love the fact that he explains the rules and Suzanne
            is meant to go, 'Okay.'

Steve: So hang on, you showed a bit of your arse? You
            turned, presumably, to show the arse?

Karl: I had to lift it up a little bit, sort of onto the draining
            board.

Steve: What did she do? Did you register her reaction?
            When she saw a bit of your arse, what happened?

Karl: When she saw my arse?

Steve: Yeah.

Karl: Well then I wasn't looking, because I thought, in a
            way, I don't want it to look like, 'Well I've seen a bit
            of your stuff, here's a bit of mine.' I just thought, at
            the end of the day, I caught a glance of you ...

Steve: ... It's only fair

Karl: You've had a bit back ...

Ricky: I think James Stewart missed a trick in *Rear Window*. That would have been a much better film, had James Stewart just popped his pants down.

Steve: It would have given a whole new meaning to the title *Rear Window*.

Karl: It's tricky though. I seem to be surrounded by people like that. Because I told you before, there's the old woman across the way who is just sat there reading a book. I look through everybody's windows like that. Remember that film, *Sliver*, when they've got video cameras? I'm just looking onto everybody's world and just seeing what people are getting up to. Nowt wrong with that.

Steve: Brilliant.

Karl: That's why I like washing up.

Thumbs and that

I'm still pretty sure that we would of got on alright without the thumb. But if we couldn't how about a thumb and one big finger.

When I was about 8, I went to school
with a couple' of kids who had big heads
and webbed hands. I don't know what was up
with em. Noone noticed they had webbed fingers for
ages cos everyone was busy lookin at the eads.
They wern't related or owt...and they didn't knock
about together. I don't think they knocked about
together cos that would of been too obvious.

They had webbed hands and it never seemed to bother em. They never seemed to have any problems gettin on with stuff. I put this down to the fact that this is all they had been used to innit.

Their skin was hard which mean't their hands
were probably more usefull than normal ones.
This is why I think we would be alright if we
only had one finger and a thumb.

I remember when I was in Wales on holiday.
Me mam and dads mates Joan and Tony were
with us. I got in from the arcade, and Joan said
"do you want a sausage roll cos there's one in the oven"
I went and picked it up. She didn't tell me she had
only just turned the oven off so the plate was dead hot
and stuck to me hand and I shuck it off and me skin
come off. This wouldn't of happened to the big headed kids cos their hands
could take it cos they were like built in oven gloves.

I got chicken pox during the same holiday. I still would of been able to scratch em with one thumb and a big finger and it wouldn't of stopped me playing on the arcade machines either.

'He just liked boats and stuff.'

Steve: Don't know if you know this, Karl, but apparently octopuses' testicles are located in their heads.

Karl: No. But to me that isn't that amazing, 'cos at the end of the day an octopus, all it is is an 'ead.

Ricky: So everything it's got has to be in the head.

Karl: It has to be in the head. It'd look daft if they dangled down below, right.

Steve: 'It'd look daft if they dangled down below.' That could almost be the B-side to ...

Ricky: ... 'I Could Eat a Knob at Night'?

Steve: Karl, the question's been asked; if you could be anyone in the world, who would it be?

Karl: Dead or alive?

Ricky: Why would you choose to be a dead person?

Karl: No, but sometimes there's people who are now dead but everybody raves about 'em.

Ricky: The idea is you choose one to live that life, not to have been that person. Are you saying that if you chose Napoleon, you would be Napoleon but you'd be back to life, walking round now, going on the bus? Or would it be the eighteenth century? What are you saying?

Karl: What I mean is ...

Ricky: Oh just answer the question. Who would you be and why? Someone you admire or you think had a good life. Just answer the question.

Karl: Well what I mean is, it's good to be remembered, like Winston Churchill is remembered as being a decent bloke, but I wouldn't want the hassle that he had, so I don't want to live his life.

Ricky: You'd like to be Winston Churchill but you'd like to have a paper round instead of ...

Steve: ... Saving the world.

Ricky: Yeah.

Karl: That's what I mean. But are you saying, 'Whose job would I wanna take on?'

Ricky It's not that complicated.

Steve: The question is this, 'If you could be anyone in the world, who would you be?' That's the question.

Karl: A lot of responsibility on a lot of jobs, in't there?

Steve: What are some of the names flowing through your head now?

Karl: Erm ... I was thinking Bruce Willis.

Ricky laughs.

Ricky: I never expected that, I never expected that.

Steve: So his responsibility, in your mind, is what? Saving people who are trapped in a building with terrorists?

Karl: Well yeah, maybe. His worries are different worries. With people who have a lot of money come other worries, d'you know what I mean? So Bruce Willis – he's always going on these marches isn't he – saying, 'stop war' and all that?

Ricky: I don't know.

Karl: ... Because he has got more to lose if there's a war. He's got loads of houses. One of 'em's gonna get damaged. Whereas if you're poor, you've only got the one house. If there's a war it's, 'Just end it all for me then. I'm sick of it anyway.' D'you know what I mean?

Steve: Whereas Bruce ...

Karl: With a successful life and a happy life there's more for you to lose is what I'm saying. Like, at the moment, I've finished the job that I've been at for ten years, right. I have finished working there, so suddenly my timetable's a bit out and I haven't got enough of a routine. And I'm a man who likes to know what I'm doing.

Steve: 'Five until seven, washing up with no thumbs.'

Karl: I've sort of turned into, like, an old person, where the little jobs that you shouldn't enjoy are now the main event.

Ricky: How old are you? You're thirty-one aren't you?

Karl: Thirty-two.

Ricky: Thirty-two and you're pottering around, not knowing what to do with yourself.

Karl: Well like yesterday, Suzanne's shoes needed to go to the cobblers, right.

Ricky: I haven't heard the word 'cobblers' for years.

Steve: I didn't know cobblers still existed.

Ricky: You only ever see them in Christmas films made by Disney.

Steve: Last time you were going to the toffee shop and now you're going to the cobblers. Next week it's the candlestick maker.

Karl: But all I mean is, suddenly that's a nice little day out. I'm sort of putting me coat on, going, 'Right, I'll go and see the cobbler now and have a chat.'

Steve: You didn't come back with three magic beans did you?

Ricky: Tell me about the cobbler.

Karl: The cobbler's alright. He's fixing shoes and that.

Ricky: He's cobbling. He's cobbling all day.

Karl: Have I told you about me Uncle Alf, who was a cobbler?

Ricky: No.

Karl: I'm sure I told you about him. He's the one who lived in a bedsit and he had two tellies. He had one that the sound didn't work on, and one that the picture didn't, but both together it worked. So as long as he was watching the same channel on both, sound came out of one telly and he would watch the picture on the other.

Ricky: Brilliant.

Karl: And he slept in a rubber dinghy. But anyway ...

Steve: Whoa, you can't just let that slide. Why did he sleep in a rubber dinghy?

Karl: He just liked boats and stuff.

Ricky: Yeah, I like boats but they're better on the water. Beds are better to sleep on. Boats are better to sail on.

Karl: Well he just had it in there. It's a bedsit. It was really tight on space.

Ricky: Boatsit? He'd moved into a 'dinghy-sit'.

Karl: He's got this dinghy, so he's thinking, 'Rather than it get in the way, I might as well use it.' But he was a cobbler and he used to repair my shoes but he would always sort of overdo 'em, right.

Ricky: What do you mean?

Karl: Like, do you know *Pimp My Ride* on MTV?

Ricky: Yeah.

Karl: Because he does up shoes, he'd go mental on 'em.

Ricky: What do you mean? There was a stereo, there was horns. "Nanana nah nah ..."

Steve: Go-faster stripes down the side.

Ricky: 'Here comes Mr Pilkington. He's got the fastest shoes in the land.'

Karl: He just made shoes that would last forever, so instead of putting one sole on, he'd put about five on so it looked like one of them built up shoes that you never see. He would just put loads of stuff on. They'd last forever.

Steve: But they did look like orthopaedic shoes?

Karl: Yeah, suddenly I was six foot seven, whenever he sort of sorted me shoes out. But he's a cobbler and it's work that's always there for you, innit?

Ricky: I suppose so.

Steve: So you went out to take Suzanne's shoes to the cobblers ...

Karl: Yeah, so I just took 'em to the cobblers and that, and that was a nice little job for the day. I got a leaflet through the door saying if you want to walk a dog, the rates are good. I don't know what they pay but I got a letter in my little letterbox saying if you are free in the day ...

Ricky: What, they pay you to walk a dog?

Karl: They pay you to walk a dog and that, and I thought if I do that and get a paper round – two in one.

Ricky: Sorry, you just went from a job where you were the Head of Production at a radio station to ...

Karl: Well, it was an alright wage but I wasn't happy, so it's pointless innit?

Ricky: I know that, but to go from the head of a department on a lot of money to walking dogs and doing a paper round ...

Karl: I know but it's about being happy innit?

Ricky: I know, that's commendable if that's true ...

Steve: ... And that makes you happier?

Karl: Well I haven't walked the dog yet but I'm just saying, if I do ... I mean I'm not taking it if it's raining. I'm just thinking if it's a nice sunny day and I fancy a potter, I'll go round to her and say, 'Well how much are you paying, I'll take the dog for a walk.'

Steve: Sure.

Ricky: But I can't believe some of the words that have cropped up. It's 2006 now: 'potter', 'cobblers', 'toffee shop'. It's very very strange.

Steve: Do you live in Narnia?

.A STORY ME MAM USED TO TELL ME.

IT WAS A STORY
ABOUT A KID WHO GOT
BORED WITH HIS PET
DOG AS IT WAS OLD
AND WASNT MUCH
FUN TO PLAY WITH.

THE KID SAID HE
WASNT GONNA PLAY WITH
THE DOG ANYMORE, AND
SAID HE WANTED A NEW
PUPPY FOR HIS BIRTHDAY

THE KID GOT HIS
OWN WAY AND
WAS BOUGHT A
BRAND NEW
PUPPY

YAP YAP

HE WANTED TO TAKE
HIS NEW DOG FOR
A WALK STRAIGHT
AWAY

YAP
YAP

BUT THE KIDS
DAD SAID IF HE
WAS GOING TO THE
PARK, HE MUST
TAKE THE OLD DOG
WITH HIM AS IT STILL
NEEDED TO BE WALKED.

HE TOOK THE OLD DOG
BUT HE ONLY PLAYED
WITH THE NEW PUPPY COS
THE OLD DOG WAS BORING
AND NO FUN.

C'MON
BOY, C'MON

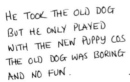

THE KID THROUGH
A STICK FOR THE PUPPY
WHICH BOUNCED OFF THE
GRASS INTO THE LAKE

THE KID JUMPED INTO THE LAKE
TO SAVE THE PUPPY, EVEN
THOUGH HE COULDNT SWIM!

HELP!

YAP!
YAP!

THE OLD BORING DOG
SAW THAT THE KID AND
THE PUPPY WERE IN
TROUBLE AND WENT TO
HELP.

AFTER THAT DAY, THE KID KNEN THAT HE SHOULD LOVE THE OLD DOG AS MUCH AS THE PUPPY.

'Would you say he's a bright bloke?'

Karl: I'm getting a lot of stuff about philosophy.

Ricky: Oh yes?

Karl: Descartes, that's one that's mentioned.

Ricky: Descartes the French philosopher?

Karl: Yeah.

Ricky: What's your question?

Karl: Someone said, 'What do you think of him?' and I was like, 'Oh I don't know.'

Ricky: He famously pondered his own existence. '*Cogito, ergo sum*' – 'I think, therefore I am'. He was thinking, 'How do I know all this is true, everything around me?' and he thought, 'Well I can see it and I can smell it and I can hear it' and he went, 'Oh yeah but my senses can be fooled. I could be dreaming' and he thought, 'Well that's true, I could be dreaming, but if I'm dreaming then at least I'm alive, at least I have some sort of consciousness, so if I am even thinking about anything, I am, I exist.' 'I think therefore I am'. '*Cogito, ergo sum.*'

Karl: But we don't need to know the Latin bit. Why is everyone always going back to Latin? It was ages ago.

Ricky laughs.

Karl: Were Latin people always in a rush, because there seemed to be, like, words for full sentences. Why couldn't they just take their time and say what they wanted to say? It's just like, 'What was the rush?'

Ricky: I'd love you to teach Latin.

Karl: What about Plato?

Ricky: Right, he's Greek.

Karl: Would you say he's a bright bloke?

Ricky: Yes I would. I would say he's a very very bright bloke.

Karl: Right, let me tell you this, right. If he's that bright, d'you know how he got killed?

Ricky: No.

Karl: Got hit on the head by an egg.

Ricky laughs.

Ricky: He's not so clever then is he? Boooo ...

Steve: What's the story with the egg?

Karl: He was on holiday or something, right, and ...

Steve: He was on holiday?

Ricky: In Greece probably.

Karl: He was having a walk about and a bird was flying over his head.

Ricky: This bird was what – a great auk? What size bird killed him with an egg?

Karl: It was a big one, yeah.

Ricky: Was it? Was it an ostrich on a hang-glider?

Karl: The way birds used to crack the eggs open to let the kids out, they used to drop 'em on rocks.

Ricky: What bird is this, dropping its egg to let the kids out? You are a maniac.

Karl: And Plato had a little bald head. So from the top, the bird's there looking down, and it goes, 'Oh there's a little rock, I'll drop the egg.' It hit him on the head – killed him.

Ricky: I'm letting too much go now because I am so desensitised to this nonsense. The bird saw Plato and said, 'There's a rock down there'?

Karl: Yeah.

Steve: Well if these birds are killing people with bald heads, you've got to be terrified.

Karl: But listen, this is what I am saying before about knowledge and that – how knowledge is hassle – or success is hassle.

Ricky: Now I think that was Newton – 'Knowledge is hassle.'

Steve: But why has Plato's intelligence got anything to do with the fact that this bird dropped its egg?

Karl: Because he was intelligent and he is probably earning a nice few quid by giving out whatever messages he gave out, he could afford to go on holiday to exotic places. If he was working in a factory, he wouldn't have been on this beach with big birds dropping eggs, so in a way it backfired. His knowledge killed him.

Ricky: And I think that was Kierkegaard – 'His knowledge killed him.'

Steve: Where have you got this stuff about him being on holiday?

Karl: Well he was. He shouldn't have been on the beach. He was only there having a break from doing what he does. It wouldn't have happened if he wasn't on holiday.

Me best Holiday

I went on quite a few holidays as a kid.

One of me favourites was to a
holiday camp in Cornwall. Me dad
got a puncture on the way there.
We went with cousins and friends
of the family. One of me cousins
carried a motorbike helmet
around with him even though he
didn't have a motorbike. He really wanted
one but his wife said they were dangerous.

We had two caravans next to each other. Our caravan tipped up if
everyone was in one end so we had to stay in groups which
thinkin about it, was a good idea.

I remember I had a problem with
me eyes on that holiday. The window
next to me bunkbed didn't shut
properly so the wind used to come in
on me eyes. I would wake up in the
morning and me eyes would be stuck
together. Me mam had to put vasaline
on me eyes before i went to sleep.
Me eyelashes were so greasy the cold
wind couldn't freeze em together.

Good holiday that though.

'That's what codes are all about, innit?'

Steve: Any nicknames? Did you ever have a nickname, Karl?

Karl: Not really. I mean there was a lot of people on the estate that I grew up on. You know nicknames are big things on estates. A lot of me dad's mates had them. What their nicknames did was tell you about them. The Elephant Man is a good name because you know what you're gonna get. If someone said, 'Elephant Man's popping round in a bit', it wouldn't be a shock when he walked in. So it worked in that sort of thing. So me dad had a mate called John the Screw.

Ricky: What, he had sex a lot? Or he worked in a prison?

Karl: No he had a DIY shop.

Ricky and Steve laugh.

Karl: So you had him, right. There was Fred the Veg ...

Ricky: I assume it's because he had the same IQ as you.

Steve: Or he was in a coma.

Karl: There was me uncle, Tattoo Stan – he had loads of tattoos that he'd just done himself.

Ricky: Oh my God.

Karl: The problem was, because he did his tattoos himself, the ones on his left arm were really good because he was right handed. But on his right arm – rubbish. So there was him and there was Jimmy the Hat.

Steve: Jimmy the Hat. Did he always wear a hat?

Karl: No, he didn't. That was the point – he never wore a hat.

Ricky: That's amazing. How can you pick up on someone never wearing a hat? How would you ever notice? 'I'll tell you what, I've noticed something about Jimmy.' 'What?' 'He doesn't wear a hat.' Why was he not called 'Jimmy the Parrot' because he never carries a parrot?

Karl: That's just the way they work innit.

Ricky: 'Here comes Jimmy Three Legs. Why do you call him that?' – 'He hasn't got three legs.'

Karl: I didn't really have a nickname – apart from when you go on CB radio and you have a chat to people.

Ricky: Oh, this was a craze in the late 70s, early 80s and it was just short-band radio, wasn't it? Everyone had these little CB hand-sets and they would speak to each other in their local area.

Karl: Yes, I think it started off with truckers. So I had one of them and me handle ...

Ricky: 'Handle' was your nickname?

Karl: Yes there's loads of code stuff. I had a couple of 'handles'. There was 'Pilkie 01' because there's a lot of Pilkingtons in Manchester so I just thought, 'Give it a number.' And then because I did boxing and that ...

Ricky: Well you did it once.

Karl: ... I had 'Boxer Boy' because that's quite a good image as well. People will be going, 'Oh don't mess with him.'

Ricky: What is the point of this?

Karl: Well you just meet people don't you?

Ricky: But you don't meet people do you? You just say, 'What's your handle?' 'Boxer Boy, what's yours?' 'Rubber duck.' 'Alright, cheers.'

Karl: Oh, but then you'll say like, 'What's your twenty?'

Ricky: What does that mean?

Karl: Where are you?

Ricky: Why don't you say, 'Where are you?'

Karl: Well just in case there is someone who is listening in. You hear about this all the time, people listening in and jotting stuff down.

Ricky: Oh right, so just in case someone in the world doesn't know what 'handle' means, they are out of the loop.

Steve: It's not a difficult code to crack is it, if you are trying to track someone?

Ricky: It's hardly the head of the mafia talking to each other because the FBI are on the wire. 'He keeps saying "What's your handle?" and they come back with something else. I can't work out what's going on.'

Karl: That's what codes are all about, innit?

Ricky: Go on then, tell me the code.

Steve: Reveal at long last to the world what these codes are.

Karl: Alright, so 'What's your twenty?' – where are you?

Ricky: This is better than the Enigma machine.

Karl: 'How many candles are you burning?' – how old are you?

Ricky: How many candles are you burning – of course. So what's the answer?

Karl: You go ... erm ...

Ricky: 'I'm fifteen.'

Karl: fourteen.

Ricky: Brilliant. There is no one that's going to work that one out.

Steve: So let's just play through this conversation. Give us an example of how it worked, because I want to hear the fascinating conversations that Karl must have had.

Karl: So you turn it on and you start off and it was something like, 'Breaker breaker, do you copy' or whatever and then you go, 'Right. It's Boxer Boy here.' And they go, 'What's your twenty?' and you go, 'Well I am just in Manchester ...'

Steve: '... In the flat ...'

Karl: And you go, 'Right, yeah, how many candles are you burning?' and you go 'I'm thirteen.'

Steve: And that's the end, is it?

Karl: Then you might sort of say something like, 'What am I burning?', right ...

Ricky   So you're 'burning' again?

Steve: Confusing but go on ... 'What am I burning?' 'The bacon, 'cos I'm busy talking to you, you twat.'

Karl: That's like, 'What's me power? What strength am I coming in at?' Because then you can tell if they're quite close to you.

Ricky: But you've just told them. They've said, 'What's your twenty?' and you go, 'I'm in Macclesfield Street.'

Karl: But then you say, 'Oh that's interesting 'cos you're burning three. I don't normally get a three.'

Steve: The least interesting thing you could ever say.

Ricky: I wish you'd have kept a diary of this because this has been fascinating.

Karl: Now and again someone will come in and go, 'Side on.'

Ricky: What does that mean?

Karl: That means there is someone sat there listening in to this chat and going, 'This sounds interesting.'

Steve: Unlikely.

Karl: And they want to join in, so they sort of go, 'Side on,' you go, 'Side on, bring it in' and they go, 'Alright.'

Steve: 'How many candles you burning? What's your twenty ...?" It seems to me that what you should have done is made a note the first time round so that when you speak to them again you don't need to ask them those questions. Instead you could just say, 'Can I just confirm that you're burning fifteen?'

'So the rocket goes off, right ...'

Karl: What we're doing here is, right, just giving you a bit of Monkey News that's gone on, right. Where a monkey has been involved in it. Good little story and that. Are you familiar with the one that went into space? The first sort of thing they ever sent up there, before man did it and all that. You see this is what annoyed me with it really. Armstrong gets all the glory, but do you know who went up there before him?

Steve: A monkey?

Karl: Yeah.

Ricky: A dog went up first.

Steve: But what was the monkey called?

Karl: Err, I don't know.

Steve: Right, okay. So it's not the most informed news bulletin?

Ricky: The dog was called Laika.

Karl: Was it?

Ricky: Yeah. They couldn't get it back though. They sent it up there, did a few tests and stuff, and they couldn't get it back. They didn't have the technology to bring the dog back because of course it couldn't fly the capsule back. Brilliant. We could all do that.

Karl: Right, well this was the next one up then, right – so the dog must have gone first and they went, 'Right we made an error there, right. Get the monkey in.' And what happened is they taught it what buttons to hit at the time that it needed to hit 'em and the way they did it was, like, give it bananas. It was like, 'Hit the red button' and it hit the red button and they'd give it a banana. And they would go, 'Right, reverse is the green one, hit the green one' and then he would do that and they would go 'There's a banana.' So it was taking commands on headphones.

Ricky: Right, but how were they giving it the banana?

Karl: No, this is before it went. You wouldn't just put a monkey in it and go 'There you go. Get on with it.' They'd sort of put him in one of them training capsules that you get.

Ricky: Yeah. I don't believe this happened. I don't think they trained it to do anything. I think they sent it up there and they put electrodes coming out of it to see how it reacted.

Karl: No, there wasn't any of that. They did a thing like they can with animals. If you give it something, like a treat, you can teach it how to do it. It's just like a dog, innit.

Ricky: It's called Pavlovian conditioning. However, that was to see if it would salivate or go over to a particular corner of the room, not if it could control a spacecraft.

Karl: It's the next step up. The monkey's not sat there going, 'Oh, I'm a bit under pressure here, it's a rocket.' All that it's knowing is, 'I am getting a banana if I hit that button.' That's all the monkey is thinking about.

Steve: But how can they be sure that it's going to press the button at the right moment?

Karl: Because it's got headphones on. They're telling it when. It's not willy-nilly.

Steve: What's to stop it just hitting the buttons at any old time because it's a monkey and it's not a human?

Karl: Because it's trained now.

Ricky: Oh it's trained? It's fully trained? Yeah, go on ...

Karl: So listen, so what happens anyway, they ...

Ricky: Oh this is absolute rubbish.

Karl: ... They popped the monkey in there. It's got its headphones on. They're going 'Right, hit the green one' and I think there's something there, a little chute, and a banana comes out ...

Ricky: No, you are making this up. There is no way that they made a spacecraft that had a banana dispenser. There is no way in this world.

Karl: So you're saying that it's easy to send summit up to
          space but you don't believe there's a little banana
          machine?

Ricky laughs.

Karl: So it comes to the launch day. Monkey is sat in
          there. Everyone is ready. Bananas are stocked up and
          all the rest of it. They go, 'Right hit the green button'
          and the rocket goes off and what have you.

Ricky: No, they would not make the monkey launch the
          rocket. Karl, you are living in a cartoon world ...

Karl: So the rocket goes off, right ...

Ricky: This is absolute bollocks.

Karl: ... It's all going well ...

Ricky: It's not going well. There is no way a monkey
            launched a rocket, you idiot.

Karl: So it's all going on and so they're going 'Hit the left
            button' and ...

Ricky: Oh, the 'left button'? Oh, well done spacecraft
            command. 'This is Houston. Hit the left button.'
            Oh brilliant. This is what happened in Apollo 13,
            they said 'Hit the left button'!

Steve: So it goes left ...?

Karl: So it goes left, heads for the moon and everything,
            and everything is going well. They get it up there, it
            does whatever it does. It reverses and it comes back.
            So then ...

Ricky: You are brain dead! I would rather have the monkey
            drive me home than you.

Karl: So the thing is, it lands back. It does a good job and
            everything. It gets out and ...

Steve: ... It's sick of bananas ...

Karl: ... This is where it turns a bit sad because after it's
            done that mission, right, because it happened and it
            was all safe and everything, the next one would have
            been to send man. But the monkey enjoyed it and it
            was like 'Well I want to do it again'.

Ricky: How did they know he wanted to do it again?

Karl: Just the way it looked.

Ricky: Ahh fuck off! 'Just the way it looked!' You are a
         maniac.

Karl: So the thing is, right, after it had done that it was on
         such a high it could never get that high again. There
         was nothing that it could do and it sort of ended
         up killing itself because it could never get that buzz
         again.

Ricky: Right. That was absolute bollocks. None of that
         is true, except that they sent a monkey into space.
         Absolute drivel.

Steve: So in your mind it committed suicide? It went on a
         crazy bender – drink and drugs and women – and
         then it was found in a motel room?

Karl: It does happen. You hear about it.

'Well, it's out there in book form.'

Steve: Karl, a lot of people are absolutely fascinated to find out how you met Suzanne, your girlfriend of how long?

Karl: Er ... ages.

Steve: And they can't comprehend how there is a woman out there for you.

Karl: Well there is someone for everyone, in't there. That's always my thing. And it's reassuring I think. You know, we've chatted about the face transplants and there's a face for everyone.

Ricky: 'There is a face for everyone.' It's philosophy isn't it?

Karl: No, there is someone for everyone no matter what condition you're in or whatever. I read an old Chinese proverb ... It's something about everyone, everything, no matter what it is, has got one talent. And that's the same way in a relationship – there's always someone out there, and that. I like the Chinese. There's another Chinese proverb that I learned – 'He who cuts the wood up, warms himself twice.'

Ricky: Yeah, that's good.

Karl: That's good, and then there's that one about too many Chinese cooks spoil the broth.

Ricky: Well I don't know who slipped the word 'Chinese' in there but I heard it as 'too many cooks spoil the broth'.

Karl: Well it was just all sort of Chinese proverbs and that.

Ricky: One of my favourites on the same subject is 'a camel is a horse designed by committee'.

Karl: What d'you mean?

Ricky: It's just a metaphor. If you wanted to design a horse and you had that vision but you let twelve people in a room have their say, it wouldn't come out as you wanted it to and it wouldn't be as good. A single vision is more perfect than a committee vision because with everyone having their say, it becomes compromised.

Steve: Rick, can I just say now – I can tell from Karl's look that he's thinking, 'Which committee designed the camel?'

Karl: Well I'd just say – why would you request the hump bit? 'Cos that's just gonna get in the way innit? I mean I've always said that about a lot of animals. It's like we've doubled up on a lot of 'em. We've chatted about elephants and mammoths. One or the other! And it's the same with a camel. I'd have that up there as 'what are they doing?' They were good years ago in the Jesus times and that. Don't need 'em now. D'you know what I mean? We've moved on.

Ricky: 'We've moved on.'

ANIMALS THAT DONT WORK THAT MUCH ANYMORE

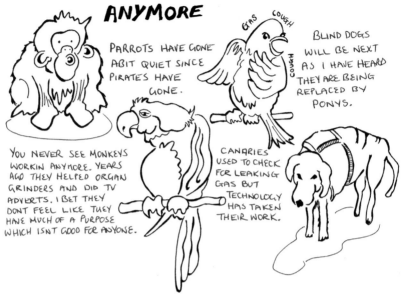

PARROTS HAVE GONE ABIT QUIET SINCE PIRATES HAVE GONE.

BLIND DOGS WILL BE NEXT AS I HAVE HEARD THEY ARE BEING REPLACED BY PONYS.

YOU NEVER SEE MONKEYS WORKIN ANYMORE. YEARS AGO THEY HELPED ORGAN GRINDERS AND DID TV ADVERTS. I BET THEY DONT FEEL LIKE THEY HAVE MUCH OF A PURPOSE WHICH ISNT GOOD FOR ANYONE.

CANARIES USED TO CHECK FOR LEAKING GAS BUT TECHNOLOGY HAS TAKEN THEIR WORK.

GAS COUGH COUGH

Steve: Not the people who use camels to cross deserts.

Ricky: I am going to throw some animals at you and you tell how you would have improved them if you'd been designing them. Okay. The octopus.

Karl: So I can now go back? I can look at 'em and go, 'What are they doing?'

Ricky: And where they've gone wrong. How could you improve it? Like the camel – you'd go, 'Lose the hump.'

Karl: With the jellyfish, I'd probably give it a bit more of a body, cut down on the arms and give it some bones, because I don't understand all this 'getting in a jar is good'. When does it want to get in a jar?

Steve: It only wants to get into a jar according to your stories.

Karl: No, but there's something that says it can get in a jar, 'cos it hasn't got any bones. But I don't know why it would want to do that in the first place.

Steve: I can't even begin to answer that. Once again, you claim that you've read that they like to get in jars. I mean, how do they know that octopuses like to get in jars?

Ricky: Okay, another animal for you then, Karl.

Steve: Giraffe?

Karl: What are they adding to the world? What are they doing?

Ricky: It's not about what they add to the world.

Karl: No, but I thought that's what everything's about. It's about 'things are here for a reason'.

Ricky: The only reason is that they survived. They passed on their genetic material and evolved and were chosen by nature.

Karl: But there seems to be a lot of ...

Ricky: The reason they are here is because they didn't die. That's it.

Karl: I'm just saying there seems to be a lot of doubling up. If I was Noah I would have gone, 'Hang on a minute, I've just seen something that looks a bit like this.' Let it drown and have a clear out. But he didn't – he was messing about saving everything.

Steve: He was instructed by God to save everything, to be fair to him.

Karl: Yeah, but if he's been given that job, for me, he's sort of manager of that job.

Ricky: So you believe Noah happened as well? And he built a boat big enough to cater for two of every species? You actually believe that as fact, do you?

Karl: Well, it's out there in book form.

Ricky: Brilliant.

Steve: You haven't answered the question that we started with. How did you meet Suzanne?

Karl: Just at work.

Steve: Thanks.

RELIGION

I JOINED THE CRUSADERS WHEN I WAS A KID BUT I ONLY DID IT COS I WAS COLLECTING BADGES AND THEY GAVE YOU A GOOD BADGE AFTER 4 WEEKS. ONCE I GOT IT I JOINED THE DENNIS THE MENACE FANCLUB. I ONLY DID CRUSADERS ON A FRIDAY NIGHT COS YOU GOT TO PLAY SNOOKER AND TABLE TENNIS. THEY PUT THE SNOOKER AND TABLE TENNIS AWAY ON A SUNDAY THOUGH AND TRIED TO GET US TO READ THE BIBLE. NO ONE EVER WENT ON A SUNDAY

LOADS OF LAND

BIG HOUSE FOR FREE

I THINK BEING A VICAR IS A GOOD JOB COS IT SEEMS LIKE AN EASY GIG. YOU NEVER SEE A STRESSED OUT VICAR.

THEY ALSO GET A DECENT PLACE TO LIVE THROWN IN WHICH NORMALLY NEXT TO THE CHURCH SO THEY DON'T HAVE ANY TRAVELLING COSTS. THE ONLY BAD THING ABOUT LIVIN WHERE THEY LIVE IS THAT THEY HAVE DEAD BODIES IN THEIR GARDEN.

THE OTHER BAD BIT OF THEIR JOB IS HAVING TO READ THE SAME BOOK OVER AND OVER AGAIN.

ME FAVOURITE STORY IN THE BIBLE IS THE ONE ABOUT THE FELLA WHO IS STRONG COS HE'S GOT LONG HAIR BUT THEN HE HAS IT CUT AND HE LOSES ALL HIS STRENGTH. I THINK HE WOULD OF LOOKED HARDER THOUGH.

THE OTHER GOOD STORY IS THE ONE WITH THE BLOKE LIVIN IN A WHALE. I WOULD OF HATED THAT. IF IT WAS A SHARK YOU COULD WAIT UNTIL SOMEONE CAUGHT IT AND CUT IT OPEN LIKE IN JAWS BUT THAT WOULDN'T HAPPEN WITH A WHALE COS NO ONE IS ALLOWED TO KILL THEM ANYMORE.

BEFORE HAIRCUT

AFTER CUT

'I know, but even if it is in a box ...'

Steve: Questions for Karl – Karl, if you could talk to any animal, which one would it be and what would you say to it?

Karl: There's a lot of stuff out there, in't there. I would probably go for the tortoise.

Ricky: Because it would take a long time to walk away from you while you were talking? Most animals would be off straightaway.

Steve: Yeah.

Karl: Just because they live for ages so they'll have loads of stories. They've lived through a lot. Through wars and stuff. If you get, like, an old one ...

Ricky: Well, most of them have lived in a box in a garden for fifty-odd years.

Karl: I know, but even if it is in a box ...

Ricky: Oh yeah, they've really travelled have they. Some of them have experienced more than you, they have broadened their horizons much more than you. They could probably teach you a thing or two, yeah.

Steve: And what would you hope to learn from them?

Karl: Just history.

Ricky laughs.

Steve: Right. From their very specific tortoise perspective?
           Other questions. If you had a time machine, Karl,
           what event in your childhood would you travel back
           to and why?

Karl: What's the point in going back to things that ...?

Ricky: Oh Jesus!

Karl: No, it's just that it's never as good is it. It's like a
           place you go on holiday and you go back thinking
           it'll be as good as the first time – it never is. So I
           don't believe in going back to places.

Ricky: What do you understand by the question? Do you think they are asking, 'Would you go back like a ghost and spy on things? Would you go back and you've got your childhood back, you are that child again? Or you're in your child body but you've got your adult head and experiences?'

Steve: Rick, I really don't think Karl was thinking there was any of those variations, let's be honest.

Ricky: I think he was thinking of himself, as he is now, in school with a cap on.

Steve: Yeah, but six foot tall sat on one of those tiny chairs.

Karl: No I don't think I would go back. It's all happened now hasn't it.

Steve: Hang on. Let's clarify one of Ricky's points. What if you could go back and you could live that moment again? How would you do it differently?

Karl: There's been times when I've gone, 'Oh that was a bit out of order' or whatever, but then you learn from your mistakes, don't you? So I don't wanna go back and change stuff, 'cos it's like that thing that they go on about where they blame the butterfly on an earthquake. You know it's gonna happen. If it wasn't that butterfly, it's another one. So why pass the buck, is what I'm saying?

Steve: So you've got no regrets? There's nothing in your past you'd want to change or do differently?

Ricky: What about if you went back and you spied on something like a ghost? You couldn't change anything but you could have a look at something.

Karl:	Like what?
Ricky:	Like Ebenezer Scrooge does with the ghost of Christmas Past. He goes back and he's looking at himself dancing and stuff. What would you do? What would you go back and have a look at?
Karl:	Yeah, but you are asking me to change. I don't wanna change.
Steve:	You're not changing – you're just observing.
Ricky:	It's impossible. It's not gonna happen. It's impossible.
Karl:	Alright. I nearly died once didn't I, on an ice-pop. Now maybe if I would have died I would say let's go back to that and I won't have an ice-pop.
Ricky:	You wouldn't be having this conversation if you'd have died. You wouldn't be having this question put to you.
Steve:	You're rewriting history and then you're going back to change it.
Ricky:	Yeah.
Steve:	There's no need. You didn't die.
Ricky:	You didn't die.

Karl sighs.

Ricky:	How can you change it? You can't change anything. You're just going to go back and watch something. Would you like to go back and watch yourself choking on a Mr Freeze?

Karl:	No, that's what I'm saying. That's why I wouldn't go back now 'cos I'm alright. I haven't had one since. I've learned a lesson. I'm not missing them ice-pops so ...
Ricky:	I don't think you are making the most of this opportunity to fantasise.
Karl:	I don't see the point of going back in anything. Do you mean go back in time to the point of you can see like, Rome, in its working day?
Ricky:	What, in your childhood? Were there gladiators in your childhood?
Karl:	Well that's what I'm saying, everything I've been through I've been through, so why see it again?
Ricky:	Forget it. Forget it. It was just a nice little question.
Steve:	I mean that shows the lack of imagination in Karl Pilkington. Your mind can't fathom something unless it's got two heads.
Karl:	But I don't see the point in doing something twice. Because the thing is – say if there's one good moment when I was about six, that I loved. I would then have to go through all the other twenty years again.
Ricky:	But why? Why have you imposed that rule? It's a fantasy. Make it up.
Steve:	Just go back and come back again.
Ricky:	Yeah, whiz back and fast forward thirty-five years.
Karl:	No.
Ricky:	Brilliant. 'No.' Like this was really on offer.

THINGS TO DO BEFORE YOU DIE

SWIMMING WITH DOLPHINS IS ALWAYS NUMBER 1 ON THE LIST. I WONDER IF ITS JUST THE LOCATION THAT MAKES PEOPLE PICK IT. IF DOLPHINS SWAM IN THE THAMES, WOULD IT BE AS POPULAR.

ALOT OF THE STUFF THAT PEOPLE WANT TO DO IS SEA RELATED. SWIMMING WITH SHARKS, SCUBA DIVING, WHALE WATCHING. I THINK THIS IS BECAUSE THIS IS WHERE WE ORIGINALLY CAME FROM AND WE STILL LIKE BEING IN IT. IM NOT A FAN COS I HEARD WE ONLY KNOW 5% OF THE STUFF THAT LURKS ABOUT DEEP DOWN. THE SEAS BIG AND HAS TOO MANY HIDING PLACES. LIKE IN SEAWEED.

SOME PEOPLE SAY THEY WANT TO GO TO THE ANTARTIC. I DONT KNOW WHY COS I HAVE SEEN IT ON THE TELLY AND IT LOOKS WELL DEPRESSING. EVEN THE PENGUINS LOOKED FED UP. I THINK IF I WAS A PENGUIN I WOULD PREFER TO BE IN THE ZOO. MAYBE THE ANTARTIC WILL GET NICER WITH ALL THESE GLOBAL WARMING PROBLEMS.

CLIMBING EVEREST IS ALSO ON THE THINGS TO DO LIST. I CAN UNDERSTAND DOING IT ONCE BUT SOME PEOPLE DO IT A FEW TIMES, WHY... NOTHING CHANGES UP THERE. ONCE YOUVE BEEN YOUVE SEEN IT, ITS LIKE THE MOON.

GALLOPING A HORSE ALONG A BEACH IS A POPULAR ONE. I GOT ON A HORSE AT A CAR BOOT SALE WHEN I WAS A KID. THE HORSE GOT OUT OF HAND AND I SLID UNDERNEATH AND GOT KICKED IN THE HEAD. I WAS TIED TO IT SO COULDNT ESCAPE. IT COULDNT GET FAR COS OF ALL THE CARS THAT WERE PARKED UP. IF IT WAS ON A BEACH IT COULD OF RAN FOR MILES SO THIS IS WHY IM NOT DOING IT.

'I said, "Look, *why are you getting involved?"*'

Steve: Another question, 'Karl, other than the famous boxing match that you have often talked about' – I know that took up about twenty minutes of your time – 'have you ever been in any other kind of fight?' I don't suppose a slanging match, I think we're talking of ever being in a physical fight.

Karl: Once that I can remember. It was over a woman. Well a girl, at school. It's hassle, innit, relationships when you're younger?

Ricky: How old were you?

Karl: About seven.

Steve: It was over a woman?

Karl: There was this girl knocking about who, you know, she was quite good looking and everybody liked, and me mate, he really liked her, and I didn't sort of ask her out and that, but she just sort of took a shine to me, and stuff, right. And I really didn't go out with her properly. It's at that age where going out with someone is just like sort of going, 'Alright' in the mornings. D'you know what I mean?

Steve: Go on.

Karl: You just sort of nod your head and that. Anyway there was some sort of school disco and they were playing spin the bottle or something, right, and I sort of wandered over to see what was going on and I stood on this girl's dress and put a hole in it. And she started crying. I was like, 'Oh I can't be doing with this' right. You know, 'What's up with you?' And everyone's going, 'Karl what are you doing? That's meant to be your girlfriend and that. You should be sort of saying, "Oh I'm sorry" and giving her a hug and all that and saying, "It'll be alright, we'll sort the dress out".' I said, 'Oh, I can't be dealing with this.' So she's crying her eyes out. I said, 'It's over.'

Ricky: 'It's over.' You saying 'Alright' in the morning? Yeah, there's no more 'Alright' in the morning.

Karl: So I go to the toilet, right, and this lad who fancies her comes in and goes, 'You're out of order.' I'm saying, 'What're you on about?'

Ricky: So there's two seven-year-olds? 'You're out of order!' 'Keep out of it.'

Steve: 'Cut it out. Show her a bit of bloody respect.'

Ricky: Sorry, were you wearing trilbys?

Steve: Yeah. He put his cigarette out in the sink and just said, 'Leave it.'

Ricky: 'Get outta my face.'

Karl: I said, 'Look, why are you getting involved?' And it was obviously because he fancied her. We had a bit of a fight in there. I accidentally sort of chipped his tooth on a sink.

Ricky: Sorry, this is like something from *Lock, Stock and Two Smoking Barrels*. What are you talking about? Two seven-year-olds in a toilet?

Steve: And you put a hole in her dress? What were you wearing – football boots? How did you make a hole in her dress? You were wearing winklepickers?

Karl: It was a dress made of like crepe, you know what I mean, it was like a crepe dress or something and that had got a hole in it.

Steve: So when you say you're having a fight, I mean are you wrestling with him, you've got arm locks and head locks going on?

Karl: A little bit of wrestling and shoving about and that
          – and it was an accident. I didn't sort of go, 'Right
          I'm going to break your teeth or anything.' It's just
          that I happened to push his head down and his tooth
          hit the sink and it chipped and what have you. After
          that I sort of left there and stuff and we had to go
          into assembly, and there was a copper in there doing
          some presentation, saying, 'Listen kids, don't get into
          trouble because we're out there and we'll get you.'
          Sort of trying to teach the young kids not to get into
          any trouble and stuff. So I'm sat in the assembly
          room, thinking, 'Oh God there's a copper here
          talking and me mate's gonna come in in a minute
          with a chipped tooth and everything.'

Steve: 'Questions are gonna get asked ...'

Karl: That's what kind of happened. I mean the coppers
          didn't get involved.

Steve: Did you turn your back on violence after that then?

Karl: That was the sort of last fight I had.

'So *what happened to him* with the beetle?'

Ricky: Karl, what do you think it's like being a crab? If you could put your mind into a crab, what would you see? Where would you be, what would you be doing? What would you be thinking? What's it like, do you think? It's like creative writing, just think, just let yourself go, come on ...

Karl: It's got to be a crab?

Ricky: What do you think of a slug? What would you do if you were transported now into a slug? You're suddenly in the kitchen but you're a slug and Suzanne's there just making tea and that. How would you let her know it's you?

Karl: It's impossible. I'd just chuck myself into the salt pot or something.

Ricky laughs.

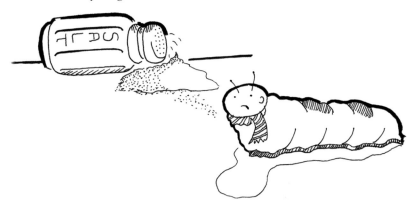

Karl: No, because what do you do? I'd hate that. That'd be horrible that.

Steve: Have you ever read Franz Kafka's *Metamorphosis*, in which a man wakes up and he's turned into a giant beetle and that's the whole story? I think it might be of interest to you.

Karl: So what happened to him with the beetle?

Steve: Well I don't want to ruin it for you in case you read it.

Karl: No I won't be reading it, don't worry.

Ricky: He joined a pop group with three other people, he was brilliant.

Steve: No, it's a really wonderful book. It's almost heart-breaking because of course, as Ricky says, he finds it very hard then to relate to other people even though he still has the consciousness of a human. His parents, the rest of his family, they don't know how to deal with him because he's a giant beetle. He becomes a freak. He becomes an outsider.

Karl: But hang on though – is he a *giant* beetle?

Ricky: Yes.

Karl: Well, yeah, that's not gonna go down well is it? Of course people aren't gonna like you. But if it's a normal sized one then you just get in with the other beetles don't you.

Ricky: How would you do that? How would you ingratiate yourself? You're suddenly a beetle but you're Karl Pilkington, right. There's other beetles, they're doing their business, they are scuttling around. And you go in there and they look at you as a new beetle. What do you do, how do you ingratiate yourself?

Karl: Well I wouldn't sort of barge into their house and that. I'd wait until they're out and about and – like in life – I'd sort of help 'em out. I don't know what beetles do all day. I have never seen one doing anything. They just seem to be going from one place to another. I have never seen 'em carrying anything. I don't know what they eat. I don't know what they do. I don't know why we've got 'em. But what I mean is, I'd watch 'em and I'd sort of help 'em out, and I mean you know, it's like going on a date or meeting a woman, innit?

Steve: Whoa, hang on. What do you mean, how is it like going on a date with a woman?

Karl: Well, it's like I said about Suzanne with her hot chocolate. She bought me that and I've gone, 'She's alright.' She gets me another one and before I know it she's living with me.

Ricky: So all these beetles, they are scrabbling around. You are watching them and then you realise that you want to mate with this female beetle. What do you do? What's your first move?

Karl: Yeah, but I don't know what beetles do, do I, so I don't know what you do. I don't know if you go up and go, 'Alright.' What do they do? How do they get on? It's a different world. I don't know yet, do I, 'cos I haven't done it.

Ricky: Would you feel bad? Having your own mind in this beetle, would you feel bad shagging a beetle? Would you think that that was a bit sick because you've got a human mind?

Karl: Well no, 'cos you'd just close your eyes and that, wouldn't you, and go 'Pretend, think of summit else.' So get round it that way. There's no point in getting down about it because I'm stuck now as a beetle, so you've got to get on with it.

Ricky: But as a slug you said you'd throw yourself in the salt pot. What would you do as a beetle if you got depressed?

Karl: No, that's what I am saying though. Beetles are different 'cos they do tend to hang about with each other. A slug is always on its own. It's a lonely insect, innit?

Ricky: It's not an insect.

Karl: Right, what is it?

Ricky: A mollusc.

Karl: Right. They're lonely. I've never seen a load of snails all together or slugs wandering about whereas beetles seem to knock about in crowds.

Ricky: Oh God.

Steve: So they're sociable creatures and it wouldn't bother you that you have got the mind of Karl Pilkington in there, because you can't communicate with these beetles because they don't speak English.

Karl: Yeah, but if it's happened to me there'll be another one in there.

Ricky: Okay, what would you do if you were suddenly a fly, right, and you were knocking about with other flies and you had to land on some excrement? What would you do?

Karl: Yeah, but I don't have to.

Ricky: What do you mean? You're a fly – you're loving it.

Karl: No, I wouldn't be loving it, would I.

Ricky: Why?

Karl: Because I'm me in that fly's head, so I don't think other flies would be going, 'Come on, join in.' I'd just be like, 'No, I'll wait here' and wait and watch and that.

Ricky: What would you do if you had to put your mind into the unhatched egg of something, like maybe one of those wasps that is injected into a spider – so you are in an egg, which is really uncomfortable, in a spider? How would you feel about that Karl? You're a baby wasp in the abdomen of a spider.

Karl: And I know everything that I know now? I'm sat in there?

Ricky: Yeah, 'Now I'm in a spider as an unborn wasp. What the fuck am I doing here? What's going on?'

Karl: I don't know what I'd do there. Err ... probably try and sleep. There's nothing else to do though is there?

Steve: I just pray to God it never happens.

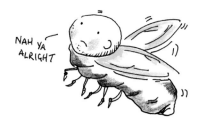

NAH YA
ALRIGHT

'It's blind and it hasn't got a mouth.'

Steve: Have you heard the famous saying of philosopher Ludwig Wittgenstein? The quote is, 'If a lion could talk we could not understand him.'

Karl: Even if he's English?

Ricky: Yes. If a lion could speak English, so there's no language barrier. He's speaking English words and using all the correct grammar and everything but you wouldn't be able to understand what he was saying.

Karl: Why?

Ricky: Because it's from a different world. Its frame of reference would be so bizarre that you wouldn't be able to get a grasp on what he was talking about because you would have so little in common, even if he used real words.

Karl: No, but he's talking English.

Ricky: Yeah, I know but his reference points would be just so far removed. You know they are removed slightly if you saw two people talking about Kierkegaard.

Karl: I wouldn't understand it.

Ricky: Exactly, so remove that a billion times to a different species with different input.

Karl: No, but it depends. If I'm talking to a lion in London zoo, he'll be saying, 'Oh I'm fed up of being stuck in here.' I'll go, 'Yeah.' It depends what its background is. I mean there's some people who might have lived down the road from me but have a totally different life.

Ricky: Absolutely.

Karl: So it doesn't matter that it's a lion. Does it?

Ricky: Well, yeah, because he has removed it even more.
          So now it's not just a bloke who lived a few doors
          away; now it's not even a bloke.

Karl: Yeah but I'd pick something smaller, you know – a
          worm, without a mouth. Then I'd go, 'Definitely
          not.'

Ricky: What? 'Definitely not' what?

Karl: I wouldn't be having a chat with it. I just think that a
          worm that's underground, what's it got to offer me?

Ricky laughs.

Karl: It's blind and it hasn't got a mouth. It's not going
          to be a good day out with it, is what I'm saying. It's
          not gonna have that much to say to me, even if it's
          English, right.

Ricky: 'Even if it's English.'

Steve: How can you tell if a worm's English? Does it wear a
          very tiny bowler hat?

Ricky: What about a jellyfish?

Karl: No. You see I think that's where you can say you
          wouldn't be able to have a good chat with 'em,
          because to me the sea might as well be another
          world.

Ricky: Yes.

Karl: In a way I think the fish sort of have more rights
          than us.

Ricky: What do you mean?

Karl: Just because, and I don't wanna slag off God, but
           if I was to have a go at him I'd say, 'You added too
           much water.'

Ricky: How would you have changed that?

Karl: Just more land.

Steve: Fair enough. Now why have fish got more rights
           than us?

Karl: Because there's loads of 'em and when you look on
           the amount of sea on the world, right, there's loads
           of that. I was in Malaga the other week, right, and
           you know you look in the sea and there's loads of
           different fish and that's just in eight foot of water. If
           you go miles out, there's like all sorts of weird fish,
           in't there, with like lights on them and everything.
           Just millions of different types.

Steve: Yeah. Now why does that mean they have got more
           rights than us?

Karl: Just because I think, you know, rights come in
           numbers don't they, if you know what I mean. Like
           if there's one of you shouting, people go, 'Oh he's
           an idiot. Shut up' or whatever. If there's loads of
           you shouting they go, 'Best listen to 'em. See what
           they've got to say.' And that's what I mean about
           fish.

Steve: Yeah, right. But they're not really making their
           voices heard though, are they, Karl?

Karl: I know, 'cos they're under water. But what I mean is
           ... I don't know what I mean.

'You see that annoys me a bit.'

Ricky: Karl, can I ask you a question?

Karl: Go on.

Ricky: I know this is what a lot of the fans are already wondering. Have you got any Monkey News?

Karl: Of course, no question.

Steve: Well I'm worried because maybe this will steal your thunder – 'Chimp mauling under investigation. Investigators said they are trying to figure out how two chimpanzees that viciously attacked a visitor at an animal sanctuary, escaped from their cage.' (This is the grim bit.) 'The chimps chewed off a man's nose and severely mauled his genitals and limbs.'

Ricky: Why did they go for his genitals?

Steve: They saw it all just dangling away and ...

Ricky: (*monkey noises*) Ah ah ah 'You go for his nose and I'll go for his bollocks' ah ah ah ah.

Karl: What happened to 'em anyway? The two guilty monkeys?

Steve: Well, unfortunately, they were shot dead by the authorities.

Karl: You see that annoys me a bit.

Steve: What are you talking about? They were attacking people's gonads!

Ricky: I know but they were happy in an African jungle a couple of years ago.

Karl: That's what they do innit.

Ricky: That is what they do. That is what animals do. Animals fight.

Steve: So what are you supposed to do – are you supposed to let them just wander off into the local mall and maybe savage some young children, or a bucket with a face painted on it?

Ricky: No, all I am saying is that you don't shoot them for doing what's natural to them.

Steve: Yes you do. If anything attacks anyone's balls.

Ricky: Were they executed or were they shot during the attack?

Steve: It just says they were shot to death. I'm assuming they shot them to death as they were legging it off.

Karl: But why aren't they just sort of tranquilised? Where was this?

Steve: Hey, why am I being accused? It's like it was my fault, just because I happen to be reading it.

Karl: It just annoys me how one day we're trying to save the pandas and then the next day someone's shooting them or whatever. I know it's not a panda ...

Steve: So therefore your argument falls apart, but go on ...

Karl: No. But I have talked about this before, about St George killing the last dragon.

Ricky: Right – it didn't exist.

Karl: It's the same thing though.

Ricky: No, there have never been any dragons – it's a mythical creature. By mythical it means – 'we made this up' – like the unicorn.

Karl: Hmm, well ...

Steve: What was your point about the dragon?

Karl: I am saying, like, why is it alright to be going around going mental with a gun shooting all the monkeys and killing 'em, because one day we are gonna run out.

Steve: What are you talking about? How have you extrapolated from this one incident of a couple of testis-happy monkeys ...

Karl: That's what I am saying. One incident. They only did it once and they've got a bullet in their head.

Steve: But they're not going around shooting monkeys and making them extinct are they?

Karl: If they carry on like this they will be.

Steve: Well then it's up to the monkeys to stop attacking people's private parts. There has got to be some give and take here, I'm sorry.

Ricky: That monkey doesn't know why it is in a cage. It's not going 'Oh this is for me own good. I'll tell you what, let's stay here because they're trying to do a nice little breeding programme here – or we could get out and do what we do best – run amok, eat some bollocks and have a good time.' Karl's right – the poor little bastards get a bullet in the head.

Karl: And for what?

Ricky: I'm saying if they are attacking a human, shoot them to stop them. That's fine. But if they are running away don't shoot them in the back like a coward.

Steve: This is an animal sanctuary, though, so presumably they had quite a kushti time there. At most of the ones I've visited the monkeys have always got it easy. They are hanging around on tyres, they've got comfy chairs, they're wanking, they're going berserk – they're loving it. So I just think there was something a bit warped in these monkeys.

Karl: But hang on a minute, you've just answered your own question there. You said they are in a sanctuary – so they haven't had a good upbringing. They're going to be a bit more, like, madder than other monkeys aren't they – 'cos that's where the ill ones go innit?

Ricky: What do you understand by 'sanctuary'?

Steve: It's not like a borstal!

Ricky: Yes, he thinks it's a borstal. He thinks they did some bad stuff in the jungle and they had a little monkey court and they went: 'Ah ah ah ah ah, send him to borstal!'

Karl: Well what is it then?

Ricky: It's a monkey sanctuary – like a haven.

Karl: Well it's not a haven is it – they got a bullet in the head!

'She's never asked for it back.'

Karl: I don't really do all that Valentine's Day stuff.

Ricky: Sure.

Karl: The problem is if you do it once, they expect it every year. That's the problem with Christmas and stuff, innit? It's become that's what you do now, every year. So I prefer to just sort of wait and if I think of an idea or I know something that she wants I might get her something, but I might not do it on Valentine's Day. It's like I've said about 'Pancake Tuesday'. Make it 'Pancake Wednesday' – have it when you want. Why am I waiting for someone to tell me when I can have a pancake? I'll have it today if I want one.

Ricky: Yeah.

Karl: D'you know what I mean? 'It's "Pancake Tuesday".' 'No, I wont bother, I'll have trifle.' So it's the same with Suzanne. Luckily, on Valentine's Day, she was ill.

Ricky: Luckily.

Karl: So we didn't have to go out. D'you want my advice?

Steve: Certainly. You may as well give it.

Karl: Treat 'em when they deserve it.

Steve: Right.

Ricky: I remember once when Suzanne was ill. She had a fever but there was no food in the house. What did you suggest to her? She was too ill to cook.

Karl: Well it was when we were still living in Manchester and we needed to get some food in for tea and I said, 'Come on, come to the supermarket.' She was like, 'No I'm ill, you go,' and I hate buying food. I just sort of get a bit blank when I'm looking at food – there's too much in't there, that's the problem?

You go down all these aisles and there's just too much. So anyway I said, 'No come on. Come with me.' She was like, 'I've got this fever. I'm hot and everything.' So I said, 'Well come to the supermarket and you go on the frozen aisle, cool yourself down.' And she did and she said it made it worse. She was ill for another three days.

Ricky: Romantic.

Steve: How would you go about chatting up a woman in a bar? What tips could you give?

Karl: I've never worked like that. It's always been a friend of a friend and all that, and just happened to meet them and then you have a chat.

Ricky: How did you meet Suzanne?

Karl: That was when I was working with her and she gave me 20p for the hot chocolate machine. She never asked for it back. I thought, 'She's alright.' That was eleven years ago, so it works.

Steve: You've never given her that 20p back?

Karl: She's never asked for it back.

Steve: And did you return the favour? Perhaps on the next date? Did you buy her a KitKat or something?

Karl: No, I don't think I did. I think word got out that she liked me and I think I did some work for her. I did some editing for her to sort of show off me skills and that, and she was like, 'Oh you're good at this aren't you.' I was like, 'Yeah,' and I think she got us another drink 'cos I was doing that editing for her in me own time.

Ricky: So you're up on the deal aren't you because I know for a fact that you've not spent any money on her in eleven years, so you're 40p up.

Steve: At least.

'No, *but nobody likes being watched and that's what I'm saying.*'

Steve: 'Migrant workers in South China are wearing adult diapers on packed trains heading home for the New Year holiday because they have got no access to the toilet. Many supermarkets in this particular part of China have reported a fifty percent increase in sales of adult nappies for the train trip.' Now what do you make of that, Karl? You're on a long, long train journey, three hours, four hours ...

Ricky: You know there's no toilet. You know you are gonna need to go.

Karl: Why isn't there any toilets?

Ricky: There just aren't, on these trains.

Karl: And they're on a really long journey?

Ricky: Yeah.

Karl: How long?

Ricky: Hours.

Steve: Very long in China. It's a big country.

Karl: I wouldn't. I couldn't do that. I couldn't do it. I'd have to hold it in or something. I mean when I was a young kid – I don't know how young you are when you wear a nappy and that – but I remember that I didn't like it, doing it in a pair of pants like that, a pair of nappies and that, and I used to have to. Even when I was too small to sort of get up on the toilet, because you'd fall in, me mam knew that I didn't like nappies and I used to just go in the corner, just near the kitchen, in this thing like a litter tray. Like cats have. It wasn't like that but that's the same sort of idea and I'd go there and I'd do me thing and me mam used to say, 'Oh he's going there. Don't look at him.' Because it put me off. You know, like cats don't like being watched when they do it.

Ricky: When they go in their litter tray in the kitchen?

Karl: No, no, they don't like it.

Ricky: What, so you were just like a little feral kid? Just running around and going in the litter tray, covering it up, and then running up the curtain and eating a sweet at the top of the pelmet?

Karl: No, but nobody likes being watched and that's what I'm saying. If you're sat on a train and you're knocking one out and that and everyone's looking at you, I don't think it'll catch on.

Ricky: Well it has caught on. They are just sitting there, reading the paper, doing Sudoku, and they're looking round as they are going and they are thinking, 'Oh no one knows I'm going.' Everyone's thinking that and everyone's going.

Steve: It's partly because there are a hundred and twenty million peasants from China's vast rural areas who swarm into the cities for work, and so that sheer number of people means that the trains are so overcrowded.

Karl: I mean what are we getting to? What's going on in the world that this is happening? I mean people have always had to travel for ages. I just don't understand why there isn't a toilet on it. We're going backwards. We're going backwards.

Ricky laughs.

Karl: Aren't we? Why isn't there a toilet on it?

Steve: Maybe there is but maybe people are thinking that the queue is going to take forever. If you have got 125 million people ...

Karl: Yeah, but not everybody wants to go at once. I mean I know the Chinese and all that are at the forefront of everything that goes on in the world, inventing stuff first, but this isn't one of the best that they've come up with.

Ricky: What have they invented then, the Chinese?

Karl: Loads of stuff, haven't they?

Ricky: Well I was just asking you. You seem quite educated on the subject.

Karl: They did them cat mop things that I told you about.

Ricky: Brilliant.

Steve: This is where you put mops on the feet of cats? Was
           that right?

Karl: Yeah, and they wander about the house, clean up
           and that. Wash the floor for you whilst they're
           pottering about. They've done, like, hats with
           umbrellas on 'em. I mean they are known for coming
           up with stuff first.

Ricky: My first thought was gunpowder. But cats with mops
           is good as well.

'I don't think they need to do that.'

Steve: I can't remember when we were discussing this but we talked about well-known phrases and quotes from the past. Karl, what do you take by the well-known saying, 'A stitch in time saves nine'?

Karl: You see, I don't think I've picked up on a lot of these sayings that have been thrown about sort of willy-nillily.

Ricky: 'Willy-nillily'?

Steve: 'Willy-nillinily', okay.

Ricky: 'Willy-nillily'!

Ricky laughs.

Ricky: But what does 'willy-nilly' mean?

Karl: Just sort of like, throwing it about all over the place.

Ricky: What do you mean? What does the term 'willy-nilly' mean?

Karl: It just sort of means, you know, care free.

Ricky: That's right, yeah. So you understood 'willy-nilly', you used a phrase. You said 'willy-nillily' but you got the gist of it, so what does 'a stitch in time saves nine' mean?

Karl: I don't know.

Steve: What do you mean you don't know?

Ricky: You must know. Think about it. 'A stitch in time saves nine.'

Karl: Is it to do with sewing?

Ricky: Well yes, sort of.

Karl: Err ... it's not that clear.

Ricky: Say if you've got a jacket, and the seam starts coming undone. 'Oh, I'll leave it. Oh, it's getting worse and worse' – soon your sleeve falls off. Initially you just needed one stitch to fix it but if you do it later you need nine stitches. And that, of course, is an analogy to other things. If you leave something that needs attention or repair it'll get worse, so do it now, do it in time.

Karl: But it depends if you're busy at that point, because if you've got something else that needs doing, that means that isn't being done because you're messing about sorting out a hole in your coat. You can't always do stuff straightaway, so I don't know if there's sort of a middle ground where you don't have to do it straightaway, 'a stitch in fifteen' or whatever. Meaning you don't have to do it straightaway but just do it before it gets really bad.

Ricky: Brilliant. Do you think yours is less poetic than 'a stitch in time saves nine'? This is what you want as a quote: 'Well, you could do it now but if you're doing summit else then don't do it immediately, but do it soon, so it doesn't get really bad' – Karl Pilkington.

Karl: But it's the same; that's the way I treat most things in life. It's like I never go to the doctors unless it's really bad.

Ricky: But that's why a lot of people die, particularly working class people, because they don't want to bother the doctor, or they are mildly embarrassed, or they don't recognise bad symptoms. Go to the doctor if you are not sure about something. Like you were terrified to go and have your prostate examined.

Karl: Still not been. Not doing it.

Ricky: Why not?

Karl: I wish you wouldn't talk about it 'cos now Suzanne will be reminded and she'll go, 'Oh yeah, you haven't been' and start dragging it up again.

Ricky: But why are you worried about a little qualified doctor ...

Karl: I don't know what they're doing up there. What year are we in?

Ricky: What are you talking about? They just pop their finger up and ...

Karl: That's what I mean though. It's 2006. Why are they still using the index finger?

Steve: Would you prefer the forefinger or the thumb?

Karl: No.

Ricky laughs.

Steve: A thumb on a stick? Some kind of thumb on a stick? A mechanical thumb? A robot thumb?

Karl: Why isn't it just a little camera?

Steve: Well, they put the camera up if they initially discover something.

Karl: Just put the camera up straightaway.

Ricky: No. They don't need to. They pop the finger up, feel that the prostate isn't swollen, and wiggle it about a little bit up your back passage.

Karl: I don't think they need to do that.

Ricky: Are you embarrassed? Are you embarrassed about being in a room with your trousers round your ankles and a little fella popping his ...

Karl: A little bit, yeah.

Ricky: Why?

Karl: And the other thing is, it's not just that, is it? You have got to go there. You're sat on the bus, stressing out, thinking, 'Oh in less than half an hour I am going to have a finger up me arse.'

Ricky: What is the problem though?

Karl: And you go in. They check your heart, and probably check your testicles and that ...

Ricky: What's up with that? They check your testicles, yeah.

Karl: Yeah, but it's all building up, and you're sat there going, 'Oh soon that'll be happening', and that's what puts me off.

Ricky: So you'd be happy if they just came round when you were asleep? Suzanne lets them in and whispers 'He's over there'. And they creep up and go bang! You'd go, 'WHAT YOU DOING!?'

Karl: I just don't understand why they don't teach you how to do it yourself.

Ricky: How can they? Imagine you, squatting in a corner with one hand on your bollocks and the other finger up your arse going, 'That seems to be alright.'

Steve: Karl, you don't understand the phrase 'a stitch in time saves nine'. I don't think you should be doing any kind of invasive medical research inside your own body.

Karl: But ... but ...

Steve: Who knows what trouble you're gonna cause?

Ricky: You would get stuck.

Steve: When Suzanne came home, your fist would be up your own arse.

Ricky laughs.

Is it worth going on the moon..

There is nowt on it so you may aswell look at it from the world, as it don't get any better the closer you get.

The moon is baron....When Neil Armstrong landed on it, he got bored after two hours and headed back home. I suppose he couldn't slag it off as they had covered his travel costs, but if he thought it was good why ain't he been back.

EUSTON..WE HAVE A PROBLEM ...THERES NOWT HERE

The moon is really old but it's got no history.
Antiques are only good when they've been used. A used plate of Henry the 8th is better than a plate owned by him that was never taken out of it's box...that's how I feel about the moon.

Go to Rome. It is nearer and more interesting

'You don't go floating about, d'you? You stay in your seat.'

Steve: Have you seen this? Virgin are plugging 'Virgin Galactic'. I think it's something like £200,000 and you'll get a chance to go in a space shuttle into space. Now I don't know what your feelings are, Rick, I know you've got a bit of cash in the bank.

Ricky: A trip into space? I don't know about that. There are things that I would spend £200,000 on as a little folly. An individual jet pack for example. I'd do that, I would like to see the earth from a couple of hundred miles up. The other thing is safety because I'm worried. I want to see a lot of people go up there first. I wouldn't have been the first bloke to go on an aeroplane. I would want to see a few pioneers go, 'It's really safe' before I got on.

Steve: Well, I believe the actress Victoria Principal is volunteering herself. I think she used to be in *Dynasty* or *Dallas*.

Ricky: Well, I'll see what happens to her.

Steve: Yeah, if Vicky P comes back alright – rather than those monkeys they sent up years ago – then we'll all be a lot more relaxed.

Ricky: Exactly. If they put electrodes on her and it all works out fine I'm interested.

Steve: There'll be a banana chute issuing bananas and there'll be buttons, 'press left', 'press right'.

Ricky: Karl, thoughts?

Karl: Go into space? It's not worth it.

Steve: Wouldn't it be a fascinating experience, to go into space and look back at the earth?

Karl: There's nowt there though, is they?

Steve: 'There's nowt there though, is they?' Say that again.

Karl: Well there's nowt there though, is they?

Steve: Right.

Karl: At what point are you meant to be happy? You're floating about up there but you don't get out, do you?

Steve: What, you mean to do some duty-free shopping?

Karl: You don't go floating about, d'you? You stay in your seat.

Steve: You want to get out into space?

Karl: Yes, but that's what I'm saying. When you go on holiday, the flight bit isn't the best bit of the holiday, is it? That's the bit you've got to do. So what I'm saying is, you've got to stay on the spaceship and then you go back home. So you don't take any luggage. I don't see the point.

Steve: You think they'll make you sit in the same clothes for the whole time?

Karl: What is the point?

Ricky: I think it's two things. I think it's the view and being able to be part of an exclusive club. 'I went into space.' It's all that about man conquering nature and you're one of that elite few that manage to pop up, see the world from a distance that no one else can see it from and then pop down.

Karl: So all that way, just for the view?

Ricky: Yes.

Karl: Is it worth it? I mean there's a lot of other places I haven't seen before I think about that. I haven't been to Scotland yet. I'm not being funny but d'you know what I mean? So just have a look in your back garden before you go looking in someone else's.

Steve: Karl, if you did go into space what would make the trip worthwhile for you?

Ricky: I know the answer, Steve. He's thinking, 'I'd like to meet some aliens that can talk like I do and I can understand 'em and they can tell me summit like "Oh, we met God, He was all right".' That's what he's gonna say. He'd like them to look like monkeys in spacesuits. That'd be his ideal thing. He'd like to go to the *Planet of the Apes*.

Karl: Yeah.

Ricky: What d'you mean, 'Yes'?

Karl: Well yeah, that'll be brilliant.

Ricky: What would be brilliant?

Karl: Seeing a little alien and that, and having a chat with
           him, find out what's been going on.

Ricky: 'What's been going on'?

Karl: No, no, but I mean if you bought me that as a
           present, right, either of you, I wouldn't be that
           happy.

Ricky: Well that's annoying because we have got you a trip
           into space – and a goat.

Karl: D'you know I am interested in going on another
           planet ...

Ricky: Karl, you are on another planet, mate.

Karl: No, no, but d'you know what I mean. It would be
           quite sort of interesting.

Ricky: How do you think you'd get there?

Karl: Well yeah, you'd go on a rocket and stuff but what
           I'm saying is, at least you know when you get there
           you're getting out, you're having a bit of a wander.
           I wouldn't be happy on just the journey bit of it,
           that's all I'm saying. I was reading about the 'Virgin

Galactic' thing and in 1971 three of 'em went up there. I can't remember their names. Wasn't the main one. Wasn't like the Buzz and the Armstrong one and that – another three blokes went up. Two wandered off, had a walk about, seeing what rocks they can find and that, and the other bloke who was left in the rocket, right, he was the loneliest man ever in the world.

Ricky: I don't know what to do. I don't know if that is some sort of profound poetry, or ...

Steve: No, stop for a moment because I just want to recapture that moment. Just say that sentence again.

Karl: Right. The other two had gone off picking up rocks, right. He's sat on his own in the rocket and he was the loneliest man in the world.

Ricky: Okay, I know what he's trying to say. He's trying to say he was the human furthest away from all other humans.

Karl: Yeah, that's what I said.

Ricky: No, you said 'loneliest'. 'Loneliest' evokes the emotion.

Steve: Yeah, it sounds like you meant he started crying and writing poetry and listening to Morrissey records.

Ricky: You mean he was the most remote man in the solar system.

Karl: Well yeah, it was saying how, like, he is on the rocket on his own and I think it turned out that the other two spacemen, picking rocks and that, were two and a half thousand miles away from him, right. So they were miles away.

Steve: Two and a half thousand miles, yes.

Ricky: But they had each other?

Karl: They had each other. He was on his own. That's weird innit? And when I hear about a weird thing that has gone on, I always think, 'What would I do?' And I was thinking about it, right; do you think that when he got up in a morning, he still bothered to put his clothes on?

Steve: That's the first thing that came into your mind?

Karl: It's just that even if me girlfriend, Suzanne, is out at work and that, I'm not happy walking about with everything out, because you never know what's gonna happen.

Ricky: What, you mean like getting it trapped in the microwave?

Karl: I just mean you never know when someone is going to turn up.

Ricky: Yes, I always pop some pants on, or a towel.

Karl: Not always.

Ricky laughs.

Karl: I've knocked on your door and you've been stood there with no pants on.

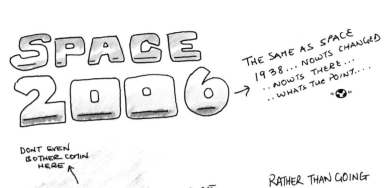

SPACE 2006

THE SAME AS SPACE
1938... NOWTS CHANGED
..NOWTS THERE...
..WHATS THE POINT....
"🌍"

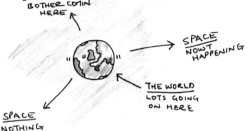

DONT EVEN
BOTHER COMIN
HERE

SPACE
NOWT
HAPPENING

THE WORLD
LOTS GOING
ON HERE

SPACE
NOTHING
HERE

RATHER THAN GOING
ALL THAT WAY,
HOW ABOUT WE PUT
A BIG MIRROR
ON THE MOON SO
WE CAN SEE HOW
THE WORLD LOOKS
FROM A DISTANCE.

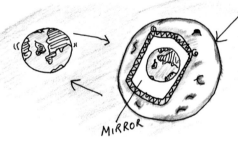

MIRROR

IF WE DID THIS, WE
WOULD NOT NEED TO
LEAVE HOME COMFORTS
TO SEE WHAT THE MOON
IS LIKE.

(TELESCOPE MAY BE NEEDED)

I DONT THINK IT IS MAD TO THINK THERE ARE OTHER TYPES
OF PEOPLE LIVIN ON OTHER PLANETS.
I LOOK AT ALIENS LIKE FOREIGNERS.

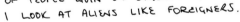

FOREIGNER (CHINESE)

DIFFERENT LOOKIN
EATS WEIRD STUFF
LIVES MILES AWAY
ADVANCED IN TECH
(ALWAYS INVENTING
STUFF THE CHINESE)

ALIEN

DIFFERENT LOOKIN
EATS WEIRD STUFF
LIVES MILES FROM MY HOUSE
ADVANCED IN TECH

(ONLY DIFFERENCE
THEY MAY HAVE
BIGGER HEADS)

'Most of them in there was that Stalin bloke.'

Ricky: I was shopping with Karl before Christmas and we went round Piccadilly and St James's and those really beautiful shops around there. I went in one shop. We had to ring a bell to enter. They came down and it's a shop that sells things from churches, nearly all Russian sixteenth century pieces. There are beautiful carvings and paintings and statues and everything, and I was wowed by it and the owner clearly loved his work, and he was enthusing to me about this stuff. 'This is from the sixteenth century. This is Russian' and I went 'Oh it's beautiful' and as I was looking round I heard Karl sidle up to the bloke and go, 'What's the newest thing you've got here?'

Steve: Sure, that's his first thought.

Ricky: I mean that is the wrong question to ask of a man who is clearly into antiques, proud of the fact that he has got sixteenth century Russian icon stuff. It's wrong to ask, 'What's the newest thing you've got here?' I mean what sort of question is that? 'Oh I don't know. Probably the door bell. Probably my shirt.' What were you thinking?

Karl: I don't know, I was just making chat with him 'cos it's the sort of place that I don't think many people go in. When you go up to this shop, right, he's not sat in there. You have to ring a bell. He's getting on with his life upstairs. He lives upstairs, right. You ring the bell to say, 'I want to come in your shop.' He pops down, stands there watching you look around. So it's not a natural way to shop.

Steve: Sure.

Karl: You know it's not nice, having a bloke stood there, watching you look at all this old stuff and that, so I was kind of making friendly chat, and I think it's an alright question, 'cos he was saying there was loads of old stuff in there. And he kept going on about the old stuff. So I thought what shall I say? 'What's the newest thing you've got.'

Ricky: Do you know the other question that he asked him? He said, 'How often do you get new stuff in?' and the bloke went 'Erm ... every day.' And I said to Karl, 'Why did you ask that?' and he said, 'Well I was thinking, if you've got antiques and you sell them all, what's left? Because they're not making any new antiques.'

Karl: But I know for a fact no one is ever gonna go in there and buy the lot anyway. I mean I've never seen anything like it. Not at any point in my life will I go, 'I need some old Russian wood.'

Ricky: It was brilliant, Steve, it was beautiful. It's amazing stuff. Carvings from the sixteenth century of saints and monks ...

Karl: There's loads of it. It's just all piled up. No one's interested. If I was him I would go, 'D'you know what, I'm into this but no one else is. Close shop.' Because seriously it's just piled up. Piles on piles of old bits of wood with pictures on it and that.

Ricky: Just think of the men 400 years ago that carved these beautiful things.

Karl: Nobody wants it do they? I've never heard anyone say, 'You know it's my birthday coming up. I tell you what I'd love – a bit of old Russian wood.' It doesn't happen. I have never overheard someone saying, 'You don't know where the Russian wood shop is do you?' And this is in London where the rates are high. There was loads of bits of wood with, like, them old drawings like. Most of them in there was that Stalin bloke.

Ricky: Right, can I just stop you there. It was Lenin.

Karl: Alright then. So he was on all these bits of wood and stuff. But I saw this other little face, right. Little fella with a beard. So, I said, 'Who's this bloke here?' He said, 'Oh the story there is this little fella who went a bit mad' or something. He got mugged back in Russia.

Ricky laughs.

Ricky: Imagine that on a sixteenth century Russian carving! 'Oh no I've been happy slapped.'

Karl: And he said, 'I've had enough of this', right, and he went to live in the woods. Made a little shed, stayed there. People went to visit him and if you've got a problem you knock on his door and you go, 'I'm sick of it' and he'd say, 'Yeah I know what you mean. I've moved out of the city' and what have you, and he'd make 'em feel better, and then they go away. Now why has that man got a plaque? If he was around now, there is no way he'd have a bit of wood with his face on it. If someone had got fed up with living in London or New York and they go, 'I'm gonna go and live in the woods' people wouldn't visit him. And he wouldn't get a piece of wood with his face on. But this man is selling it for about £750 – for this bloke's head! He's having a laugh.

Ricky: Because it is 400 years old and beautifully painted.

Steve: The chances are that this is either a well known Russian folk tale or it may even be a piece of classic Russian literature.

Ricky: Or he's a saint.

Karl: Everybody was a saint years ago. Who's a saint now, in this year? Name me one now? Yet this fella lived in the woods in a hut. 'Oh yeah, that's Saint John' or whatever. He's not a saint. He's done nothing. If anything he said, 'I can't be bothered with living in the city with everyone else. Everyone else has got to put up with it but I can't put up with it, I'm gonna live in the woods.' Well if you can't put up with it, you're not good enough, are you? You've got no stamina. And yet he gets a plaque, is what I'm saying. It's annoying.

Steve: Who would you like to see get a plaque in the modern world? Who deserves a plaque in your opinion?

Karl: Probably like nurses and that, who do a lot of bad things, that I couldn't do that, like carrying lungs about and all that.

Ricky and Steve laugh.

Karl: Me mam wanted me to be a doctor.

Ricky: What? What was she thinking? When did she start
        giving up on that dream? At what age did she start
        going, 'Karl you don't need to study your books any
        more. Go and play with the worms in the garden?'
        When did she let you off that dream?

Steve: Was it the day she caught you with a spoon up your
        nose?

Ricky laughs.

'So *he was a bit of a hoarder?*'

Steve: A reminder of Ben Franklin's famous mantra 'waste not, want not'. Karl, do you have any personal mantras you could pass along?

Karl: Who said that?

Steve: Ben Franklin.

Karl: What was he? What did he do? What was his job?

Steve: Benjamin Franklin was a well-respected American politician from the 1800s. He was a thinker, a philosopher, a scientist. Deeply respected.

Ricky: He's on American money.

Steve: He's on a dollar bill or something. So he is one of the great American enlightenment thinkers and he came up with the mantra 'waste not, want not'.

Karl: What does it mean?

Steve: You've never heard that?

Ricky: Don't throw stuff away because you might need it and you won't be wanting for anything if you don't throw it away.

Karl: So he was a bit of a hoarder?

Ricky: Yes, he was a bit of a hoarder.

Steve: For God's sake.

Karl: I am just saying, you know, he's a man in power, is that the best thing he's ever said?

Steve: No, I'm sure he came up with many profound things. He did experiments in electricity, in conducting electricity and all sorts.

Karl: But that impresses me more, inventing electricity, than someone ...

Steve: He didn't 'invent electricity'.

Ricky: Impresses you more than what?

Karl: Just saying, 'waste not, want not'. I don't think it's that good. It's not even catchy. What I don't understand is why he was the first person to suggest, 'Look don't go chucking that out, keep it, you might need it later.'

Ricky: Say that again. That is brilliant. Now why hasn't that caught on? That's poetry. How would you word it?

Karl: I'd just say, 'Whoa, whoa, don't be chucking that out. You might need that later.'

Ricky: 'Don't be chucking that out, you might need that later', Karl Pilkington, 2005.

Steve: 'Waste not, want not' is perhaps a little more pithy.

Ricky: We should go through the great sayings and phrases with Karl.

Steve: Firstly, does he know what they mean? And secondly, can he improve them?

Ricky: Winston Churchill: 'Never have so few done so much for so many.' What do you think of that? Do you know what that means?

Steve: It's with regard to the Battle of Britain and the pilots that gave their lives.

Karl: If I was one of them men who gave up his life, right, I'd want a name check. I don't want to be bungled in with everyone else in this 'A load of blokes gave their lives, well done and that, see you later.'

Steve: Did you just say, 'Bungled in'?

Karl: Yeah, bungled in, yeah.

Ricky: You made up a word. That's it you see. We've been looking for that. That's original, that's Karl Pilkington. 'I don't wanna be bungled in.'

'No, *no I was looking at another one.*'

Ricky: Karl, you hate nudists, don't you?

Karl: Nudists. I don't understand what it's all about at the end of the day – and here's something, right – do you ever get any bloke nudists who have a small knob?

Ricky: I don't understand the question.

Karl: Are there any blokes who are knocking about who just have a normal size knob – or maybe a bit smaller than a normal – who are happy wandering about showing off what they haven't got ... if you know what I mean.

Ricky: I don't think nudists are just doing it because they are proud of their knobs.

Karl: No, but there's got to be a little bit of that in it, in't there? You know Jonathan Ross, right, and he's always happy getting his knob out, 'cos he's known to have this big knob, right.

Ricky: What do you mean, 'he's known?' Why is Jonathan Ross known to have this big knob?

Karl: No, he just talks about it a lot, doesn't he? He's always saying, 'Oh I bet you'd like this wouldn't you', and all that.

Steve: But that's like me saying I'm known for being a great lover. I say it a lot, it's clearly not the case. What evidence have you got that he's got a big knob?

Karl: I saw it ... Well, no, he did get it out but I wasn't looking ...

Ricky: What do you mean 'You weren't looking'? How would you know it was out?

Karl: Just because he was sort of moving it about and that, and I could sort of see. No, I wasn't looking though. It was that sort of thing when you can see something moving about but you're like, 'I'm not looking at it.'

Ricky: What, like an owl seeing a mouse?

Karl: It doesn't matter. All I'm saying is ...

Ricky: No no no, let's get back to you remembering, vividly, Jonathan Ross's penis.

Karl: No. I don't mean that.

Ricky: Why were you looking at his penis ...?

Karl: I wasn't looking.

Ricky: ... When it was clearly not meant to be looked at.

Karl: I'm just saying, most blokes who are nudists, they must be pretty confident in themselves to get it out. And I wasn't looking, it is just that ... I mean I looked once.

Steve: What, sorry, you looked at Jonathan's once?

Karl: No, no I was looking at another one.

Ricky: What, at the same time? Why are you looking at loads of men's penises?

Steve: What's going on – where are you hanging out?

Karl: It's not unusual. It's natural, that's what I'm saying.

Ricky: What do you mean? What are you looking at? 'Karl takes a sneaky look at men's-cocks.com'

Karl: No, what I'm saying is – it's natural.

Steve: Where was this happening? So you were in a gym, a lot of guys were getting changed and you were just checking out their knobs?

Ricky: No, you were at your bedroom window with a pair of binoculars and there was a little fella across the road getting changed?

Karl: No, I was at some night out once, right, and some people come running on the stage, right. Some music started coming on and these four people ran out. There's two women and two blokes.

Steve: So you were at a gay strip club?

Karl: It wasn't gay. It was just a normal night out. Well you know, some sort of party night out. These people come running on. You got two women. You got two blokes. They whipped their knickers off and the fellas whipped their undies off.

Ricky: At the same time?

Karl: Yeah, all at the same time.

Ricky: Was it like a choreographed thing?

Karl: Like, whatsit, erm ...

Steve: The Chippendales?

Karl: No, you know – Cheryl Baker was in it.

Ricky: Oh, 'Making Your Mind Up' with Bucks Fizz. A larger skirt concealing a smaller skirt. At no point did Bucks Fizz whip their knickers and pants off.

Steve: When you said Cheryl Baker was in it I was thinking, 'Didn't she used to host *Record Breakers*? I don't remember that on at tea time on BBC l.'

Karl: So that happened, and all I'm saying is before I had a look at the women's bits, right, I just had a little cheeky glance at the fellas'.

Ricky: Why?

Steve: Why?

Karl: Just checking it out. Just seeing if everything is normal down there.

Steve: Why weren't your eyes drawn instantly to the ladies' bits?

Karl: No, believe me, I had a look at that. All I'm saying is ...

Steve: But you went to the guys' first?

Karl: I didn't know how long the pants were gonna be left off for.

Steve: And you didn't want to miss the opportunity? You saw an opportunity to see some men's bits and you thought, 'I'd better take it 'cos this may never happen again.'

Ricky: So what happened? There's two women, two men, right. I don't know what sort of event this is where you are all looking at people getting their knickers and pants off. I don't know why you're looking at all.

Karl: Good night out.

Ricky: So you think, 'Right, there's knickers and pants off – let's check out the knob and testicles first.'

Karl: You're telling me when you've been in a gym or something you have not just turned your head, had a look and gone 'Oh, right, yeah that's alright, yeah.'

Steve: Sorry, let's just get this question right. Have we ever been in a gym and just taken a sneaky glance at a man's genitals? Is that your question to us?

Karl: Right, for me it's the same as when you see someone who is a bit odd – two heads or whatever.

Ricky: Well, I'll be honest. If I was in a gym and a bloke came in with two heads, I would look. I would get a sneaky glance in the mirror.

Steve: But would you look at his genitals or his two heads? Or would you sneakily look at the heads and then think, 'I wonder if he's got two cocks?'

Ricky: I tell you what – and I admit it – if I am ever in a gym and a naked man with two heads walks in I would probably check out the genitals as well, just to make sure that he's got two of everything.

MY TOP FIVE FREAKS

THE ELEPHANT MAN IS
PROBABLY THE MOST FAMOUS FREAK
OF THEM ALL.
I FOUND OUT RECENTLY THAT HIS
NAME WAS JOSEPH AND NOT JOHN
WHICH IS THE NAME EVERYONE
CALLED HIM.
I THINK THIS WAS THE LEAST OF HIS
WORRIES.

1. THE ELEPHANT
   MAN

THEY ARE CALLED SIAMESE TWINS
COS THATS THE AREA THE FIRST
ONE (TWO) CAME FROM.
I THINK THIS MIGHT BE THE WAY
WILL BE IN THE FUTURE. EVOLUTION
MIGHT MAKE US TWO PEOPLE IN
ONE TO SUIT THE BUSY WORLD
THAT WE LIVE IN. THIS WAY WE
CAN MULTI TASK MORE.

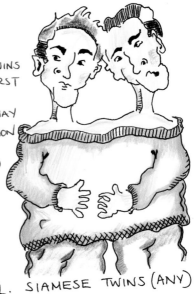

2. SIAMESE TWINS (ANY)

THE PILLOW MAN WAS IN AN OLD BLACK
AND WHITE FILM CALLED FREAKS.
IT IS ONE OF MY BEST FILMS.
THERE IS LOADS OF WEIRD STUFF IN
IT. THERE ARE SOME PEOPLE CALLED
PIN EDS, A WOMAN WITH A BEARD,
A BLOKE WITH HALF A BODY AND
THE PILLOWMAN. THERE IS A BIT
IN IT WHERE YOU SEE HIM LIGHT A
FAG USING JUST HIS MOUTH. I
THINK THIS WAS HIS PARTY TRICK
WHEN HE'S DOING THE FREAK SHOW.
IF HE GAVE UP SMOKING I DONT
KNOW WHAT HE'D DO.

3. THE PILLOW MAN

THIS IS A YOUNG BLOKE CALLED
FRANCIS. HE HAD THREE LEGS BUT
ENDED UP BEING A JUGGLER.
I DONT KNOW WHO IS CARRERS ADVISER WAS.
ITS WEIRD HOW THIS WOULD BE CLASSED AS
A DISABILITY, I THINK ITS MORE LIKE A
SUPERPOWER.
ID BE HAPPY TO HAVE THREE LEGS
BUT IT WOULD BE A BIT ANNOYING
COS I SUFFER WITH RESTLESS
LEGS SYNDROME. THIS MEANS ME
LEGS GO A BIT MAD AT NIGHT.

4. THE THREE
   LEGGED
   JUGGLER

IVE NEVER SEEN A REAL PICTURE OF
THIS ONE. IVE ONLY EVER READ ABOUT
HER. SHE WAS FROM A TIME WHEN THERE
WERE LOADS OF ODD LOOKING PEOPLE
ABOUT. YOU CAN TELL THIS BY HER NAME,
THE FACT SHE WAS CALLED THE PIG FACED
WOMAN OF MANCHESTER SQ SAYS TO ME
THERE WAS PROBABLY A PIG FACED WOMAN
ALSO KNOCKING ABOUT RUSSELL SQ.

5. THE PIG FACED WOMAN
   OF MANCHESTER SQ.

> *'So anyway they said,*
> *"Well how are we gonna*
> *get up there?"'*

Karl: This one's about a fire that happened. D'you know in New York they have loads of big buildings, don't they? Really tall ones.

Ricky: Skyscrapers?

Karl: And there was a fire in one of them, right. So they did as expected, they called up the fire brigade and that. They turned up, right. Fire engine parked up. It's like, 'Right where's the fire?' and they said, 'Oh, it's on Floor 100' or whatever, and they said, 'Oh no. We've brought the fire engine with the short ladders.'

Steve: Stupid mistake, but go on ...

Karl: Right. So anyway the fire's going and that and
          they're saying, 'Is there anyone in there?' They go,
          'I don't know. There might be someone up there but
          the telecom is not working and stuff.'

Steve: Who do you think might be up there, Rick?

Ricky: I dunno.

Steve: Just a woman I imagine – a woman or a child.

Ricky: Is there a fireman that could climb up a building
          without a ladder?

Steve: I think it's unlikely, but go on ...

Karl: So anyway they said, 'Well how are we gonna get up there?'

Steve: 'We can't, we've only brought a short ladder.'

Ricky: 'No we can't. Let's go home.' Okay, so that was Monkey News ...

Karl: So they said, 'Well there's a lot of 'grippage'.'

Steve: Because they made up words, the firemen.

Ricky: There's a lot of 'grippage.'

Karl: ... On the side of the building and stuff. So anyway they said, 'Why don't we just go and get a monkey?' right. So they got a monkey.

Steve: Whoa, that's a bit of a jump.

Ricky: Is that policy now, in the New York fire department?

Karl: Well you know you've got to think quick, haven't you? At the end of the day, if people are up there you don't start querying if it will work or not, you try everything that you can to help someone out.

Ricky: That's the first thing they thought of, was it? A monkey?

Steve: So it was quicker for them to go and get a monkey than to go back and get the long ladders?

Ricky: Why didn't they get Spiderman?

Karl: So anyway, they got a monkey down there, and they said, 'Right ...'

Ricky: Where did they get it from?

Karl: We don't know. From the local zoo or somewhere. So they said, 'Look, we've got to remember, there could be someone up there and it'll shock 'em a bit if a monkey comes in, right,' so they said, 'We'll just get it a little small uniform and that.'

Ricky: Whoa, whoa, hold on. 'Where are you going to get the uniform?' 'I'm going back to the station.' 'Well get the long ladders while you're there.' Ahh, you're an idiot.

Karl: So anyway, it goes up there. It's got all the kit on, its little hard hat on and all that. There was a little person up there and it manages to grab them ...

Steve: Who was up there then? Someone that was just the right size for a monkey to be able to rescue, which is handy because if it had been anyone else, like a larger person or a family ...

Karl: I don't know about the size of it, but the story is saying how, like, it was quite a big monkey and that. It was good at breaking down doors.

Ricky: Oh yeah.

Karl: It was good at climbing into small spaces and stuff like that.

Ricky: Oh yeah.

Karl: Anyway ...

Ricky: So it's big enough to carry a fully grown man but small enough to climb through a cat-flap?

Karl: Yeah.

Ricky: Which is handy.

Karl: So anyway, it got the person and everything and now it's on call if they ever need it again.

Steve: Sure, if they ever get anywhere again and they've forgotten the long ladders but there is plenty of 'grippage', they just call for Coco.

Karl: That's this week's Monkey News.

Ricky: Bollocks.

ANIMALS WE DONT NEED
TOP 5.

① **JELLYFISH**
THEY DONT KNOW WHAT THEY ARE DOING.. THEY JUST FLOAT ABOUT STINGING STUFF. THEY ARE 97% WATER AND THEY ARE ALWAYS IN WATER SO WHY NOT MAKE EM ANOTHER 3% WATER AND JUST MAKE EM INTO WATER.. DROUGHT SORTED.

② **COCKROACHES**
THEY CAN LIVE FOR A WEEK WITHOUT AN HEAD DONT LIKE THE IDEA THAT SOMETHING CAN LIVE WITHOUT A HEAD. I DONT KNOW WHAT BIT STAYS ALIVE THOUGH.

③ **SNAILS**
I DONT KNOW WHAT THEY DO. HAVE HEARD THAT THEY GET IN POST BOXES AND EAT STAMPS OFF LETTERS.

④ **SLOTHS**
LAZY. ITS NAME IS A WORD FOR SOMEONE WHO IS LAZY. NOT EXISTING IS LIKE BEING ASLEEP SO GET RID OF EM, THEY WONT MIND.AS LONG AS THEY DONT HAVE TO SORT IT OUT.

⑤ **PUFFA FISH**
DONT LIKE THE WAY THAT IF YOU EAT IT AND ITS NOT COOKED RIGHT, IT CAN KILL YA. WHY IS IT STILL PROTECTIN ITSELF WHEN IT IS DEAD.

THESE ARENT IN ANY ORDER, ONLY THE JELLYFISH THAT IS MY NUMBER ONE BAD ANIMAL CAN STAY IN THE ABOVE CHART POSITION.

'Do *we* need 'em?'

Karl: More animal stuff, right. When I was round your house the other night, your girlfriend Jane was talking about how they're getting closer to doing the mammoth.

Ricky: Yes, they're genetically engineering it. They are a few million bits and pieces away but they reckon they're going to be able to build a living mammoth within two years.

Steve: Really. What, sort of *Jurassic Park* type stuff?

Ricky: Sort of, yeah. What do you think of that Karl?

Karl: Do we need 'em?

Steve: What do you mean?

Karl: Well is it worth messing about? Because I always think, whoever's knocking one of these together, right, they must be pretty bright, right. So whilst they're messing about with an 'airy elephant, could they be doing more useful stuff that the world needs?

Ricky: Even if, on the face of it, it looks pointless, it's about conquering nature isn't it? I mean that's amazing, isn't it, that you could bring a mammoth back. What are the implications of bringing a mammoth back? Could they aid the workload? Could they feed the starving? There are applications.

Karl: What, so you're saying bring it back to kill it to eat it?

Ricky: Well I'm not saying anything. I'm saying that rarely is scientific discovery pointless and a waste of time in the greater scheme of things. We learn from this, the fact that we can map the DNA of a mammoth. What are the implications there? Could we bring back – I don't know – Churchill? Could we bring back Nelson? Would we want to? Is it moral? That's another question, but the feat alone ... I don't mean its feet. I don't mean we can bring back a mammoth's feet.

Steve: I could see that was the way he was thinking by the way his eyes moved.

Ricky laughs.

Ricky: Yeah. I mean the achievement alone is remarkable. Putting a man on the moon, pointless, but, what a feat ...

Karl: Don't you think ...

Ricky: Not impressed by putting a man on the moon?

Karl: No, we've chatted about the man on the moon, you know, some people like it, some don't. I'm not gonna argue about it. If you were behind it, good on you, but I'm not that fussed. I don't think we've learned that much from it. They went all that way, popped a flag up, came back. What have we learned about that journey since? We haven't really been back.

Ricky: We conquered space. That's what we do. We see what we can do. Why climb a mountain? Because it's there. What's at the bottom of the ocean?

Karl: Yeah but I don't agree with people who climb mountains for the sake of it. It's all right if you've got to get over it but don't go up and then go down again. Just go for a good walk.

Ricky: I don't mind as long as they don't strain the emergency services. If you're a posh bloke going up the mountain in a blizzard and you get stuck, you're an idiot. And then people have to risk their lives going to rescue you because you wanted a laugh. I agree with that.

Karl: But don't you think the world's busy enough? It's like you can hardly move. And mammoths are taking up quite a bit of room if a load of them come back. We've already got elephants, which in my eyes are good enough. They'll do. They carry stuff about, and that. What's going to be better, a mammoth or an elephant, 'cos I can see that one of them is going to have to go at some point. If we start running out of elephants, would they say, 'Oh it doesn't matter, we've got mammoths' and stuff?

Ricky: You don't need anyone else in the room for a conversation, do you?

Karl: No no, but ...

Steve: He's arguing with himself.

Ricky: He's arguing with his own head.

Steve: Amazing.

Karl: Where would you put the mammoth? If they get it going, right, give it the old electric shock and that, wake it up and it's ...

Ricky: He's been watching *Frankenstein*. All his information about science and history is from *The Flintstones*, *Planet of the Apes* and *Frankenstein*.

Steve: In his head they've got an elephant, they've put some carpet tiles over it and they're trying to bring that back to life as a mammoth.

Karl: Oh forget it then.

Amazing Science

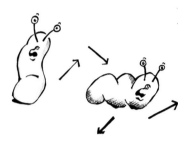

THIS IS ABOUT A TEST THEY DID ON A LEECH. THEY PUT A LEECH IN A MAZE AND PUT SOME CHICKEN BEHIND ONE OF THE BUSHES. IT WENT FOR DAYS GOING UP AND DOWN ALL THE DIFFERENT PATHS UNTIL IT FOUND IT.

WHEN IT FOUND IT, THE PEOPLE DIDN'T LET IT HAVE ALL THE CHICKEN.

THEY THEN PUT THE LEECH IN WITH A BIGGER LEECH THAT HADN'T EATEN FOR AGES. THE BIGGER LEECH BATTERED THE SMALLER LEECH.... AND ATE IT.

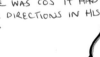
CHICKEN HID BEHIND TREE

THIS IS WHEN THE WEIRD BIT HAPPENEND. BECAUSE THE BIG LEECH HAD ATE EVERY BIT OF THE LEECH INCLUDING THE BRAIN, IT STARTED TO GET THE MEMORY OF IT.

IT GOT FLASHBACKS OF THE OTHER LEECHES LIFE AND SAW THAT THERE WAS MORE CHICKEN LEFT BEHIND THE TREE AND IT KNEW EXCACTLY WHERE THE TREE WAS COS IT HAD ALL THE DIRECTIONS IN HIS HEAD.

THIS OTHER LEECH WILL THEN EAT THIS LEECH AND THE KNOWLEDGE LIVES ON

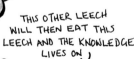

THE PEOPLE WHO DID THE TEST SAID THE LEECH FOUND THE CHICKEN STRAIGHT AWAY WITHOUT ANY MESSING ABOUT.

THIS WOULD BE GOOD IF PEOPLE COULD DO THIS WHEN MEMBERS OF THEIR FAMILY DIE. INSTEAD OF BEING SAD AT A FUNERAL, EVERYONE WOULD EAT SOME OF THE BRAIN AND LOOK BACK OVER SOME OF THE PERSONS MEMORIES.

'Well it did happen. It was in a science magazine.'

Steve: Question here: 'Karl, what would you change if you were in charge of what kids are taught in school?'

Karl: What I'd do right, instead of sort of teaching kids about two and two and that – which is four, right.

Ricky: Show off.

Karl: I think they should be asked more questions that make 'em think rather than something that has just got an answer.

Ricky: I totally agree. Teach them a desire for a quest for knowledge, inflaming their imagination.

Karl: But just freaking them out a bit as well.

Steve: I knew where that was going. As soon as you started talking, Rick, I was thinking, you're thinking of some of the big existential or philosophical questions. What does it mean to be human? What does it mean to interact with other people? Whereas ...

Ricky: He was thinking, 'freak 'em out a bit.'

Karl: Just like, you know, I read the other day that a dishwasher has been found on Mars.

Ricky: Rubbish.

Karl: So tell 'em that and say ...

Steve: But it's not true!

Karl: ... Go home and write about it. 'How did that happen?'

Ricky: But it didn't happen.

Karl: Well it did happen. It was in a science magazine.

Ricky: No, it didn't happen. There was not a dishwasher on Mars.

Karl: Why not?

Ricky: I'll tell you why not. How did it get there?

Karl: But we're always sending rubbish out there and that.

Ricky: Not dishwashers! What do you think, the council take it away and they think, 'Where can we put it?' 'Well, the tip's full, where's the nearest thing we can dump this?' 'Mars, I imagine.'

Karl: No, but the same way that fella who – I don't know, was it two Christmases ago? When he was messing about saying, 'I can get stuff to Mars' and all that. He did it wrong 'cos he did it on Boxing Day and I just think nobody's concentrating. No one wants to work on that day, they are gonna do stuff sort of half arsed, aren't they, on Boxing Day? So it didn't really get there I don't think, but it crash landed.

Steve: A probe, do you mean?

Karl: Yeah. But the thing is, it got there, didn't open properly. No one's been back to pick it up. And what I'm saying is, we're saying about going to Mars as our next planet. It's a tip! There's loads of stuff that's been fired up there.

Ricky: No, no it's not.

Karl: It has. Like that probe thing is still there, rotting away.

Ricky: So, *ipso facto*, there is a dishwasher on Mars? We've settled that. Why would they have a dishwasher on Mars? Would they take the dishwasher up in the space shuttle in case they had dinner parties?

Karl: I just think they would have a little dishwasher in there. There's a lot of them. Tight space. You don't want arguments, 'Whose gonna do the washing up?'

Ricky: Do you know how much fuel it takes to move a kilogram out of the earth's atmosphere? They're going to take up a dishwasher, are they?

Karl: How many people does it take to fly a rocket? Tell me, how many people?

Steve: Well it's either one monkey, with a banana chute that feeds it, or probably two or three humans.

Karl: Right, say it's three humans. Now there's three humans because they need one to steer it, one to be going, 'Yeah, we're alright.'

Steve: And one to make some hors d'oeuvres?

Karl: No, what I'm saying is, if you're gonna start having a sink, then whoever's washing up ...

Ricky: They haven't got a sink!

Karl: I know, 'cos they've got a dishwasher!

Steve: Ahh, he's got you there.

Karl: But anyway, I'm not gonna go into that. All I'm saying is, teach kids things, say to 'em, 'Right, when you go home tonight, there was dinosaurs knocking about ages ago, how would you have lived with them? Get on with it. See you later.'

Ricky: Well, they didn't. I've told you this before.

Karl: All right then, here's a different question. Would it be better to have dinosaurs knocking about now, whilst we're here? I put that in my diary the other day, that when you think about it, there's a population problem. There's too many of us.

Steve: Yeah.

Karl: We're saving people all the time. No-one's allowed to get injured anymore. You've got to wear a helmet when you're on a bike. There's speed bumps to slow people down. Zebra crossings. Cures for illnesses. No one's dying anymore.

Ricky: I think they are.

Karl: Not as many as there should be, because the world's crowded.

Ricky: I think there are still people dying.

Karl: Not that many though.

Ricky: Yeah I think there are still millions of people dying.

Karl: Loads of people are living longer, and that's the
          problem. So what I'm saying is ...

Steve: You think you should introduce *tyrannosaurus rex*
          into London?

Karl: Wandering around.

Steve: Just have them wandering around, just picking
          people off?

Karl: Just sort of random and that. I mean I'm not wishing
          that anyone I know dies and that, but all I'm
          saying is, I don't know anyone who's died for ages.
          Whereas if a dinosaur was knocking about, you'd
          go, 'Oh, Neil's gone missing ...'

Ricky laughs.

Karl: Whatever. I just think then it is survival of the fittest.
          We have lost all that now. You don't even have to be
          fit to survive. They just keep sticking a new lung on
          you.

.HOW I WOULD LIVE WITH DINOSAURS.

I THINK THE FIRST THING THAT I WOULD MISS IS HAVING ME WALKS.

I PROBABLY WOULDNT GO OUT AS MUCH. SO THE KNOCK ON THING THERE WOULD BE I'D GET FATTER, WHICH WOULD MEAN I AM MORE ATTRACTIVE FOR A DINOSAUR TO EAT AND I WOULDNT BE AS GOOD AT RUNNING AWAY COS I WOULD GET TIRED QUICKER.

AT THE END OF THE DAY WE LIVE WITH DANGEROUS THINGS NOW AND GET BY OKAY, WE WOULD JUST LEARN TO AVOID CERTAIN THINGS LIKE WE HAVE DONE WITH LIONS, TIGERS, RHINOS AND HIPPOS. HIPPOS ARE BAD COS THEY ARE REALLY DANGEROUS BUT NOT MANY PEOPLE KNOW THIS, AT LEAST A DINOSAUR LOOKS BAD.

IT MIGHT BRING PEOPLE TOGETHER MORE COS THATS WHAT PEOPLE DO IN TIMES OF TROUBLE. IF A CERTAIN AREA IN BRITAIN IS GETTING OUT OF HAND, YOU PUT THE DINOSAUR THERE.

I SUPPOSE WE COULD BUILD A BIG WALL.

IT MAKES ME WONDER IF THIS IS WHY ALIENS DONT VISIT US ANYMORE. MAYBE THE LAST TIME THEY CAME, DINOSAURS WERE KNOCKING ABOUT, A DINOSAUR ATE ONE OF THE ALIENS AND SINCE THEN THEY HAVE AVOIDED THE PLACE. MAYBE THE ALIEN WAS POISONOUS AND THATS WHY THE DINOSAURS DIED OUT.

IF WE KNEW YEARS AGO, WHAT WE KNEW TODAY AND WE WERE ABOUT WHEN THE DINOSAURS WERE ABOUT, I THINK WE WOULD OF SAVED THEM FROM EXTINCTION COS THATS WHAT WE DO. NO MATTER IF SOMETHING IS REALLY DANGEROUS, IF IT WAS IN DANGER OR HAD TOOTH ACHE OR INFECTION IN ITS BIG FOOT WE WOULD HELP IT COS THATS WHAT PEOPLE DO THESE DAYS..... THEY SAVE EVERYTHING.

=ROAR=

=ROAR=

'I'll start a diary'

Ricky: But Karl's been on holiday again hasn't he?

Steve: Oh yeah, that's right. Karl, you don't do anything ...

Ricky: You get weekends off, you take at least five or six weeks holiday a year – even though you haven't got a job now.

Steve: You spend your whole life on holiday basically.

Ricky: I don't know why you need a holiday. You just potter around. Your big day last week was going to the cobblers so why did you need a break this week?

Karl: It's just good for your brain and that innit? It opens it up a bit.

Steve: You're not evidence of that.

Ricky: Where did you go?

Karl: Gran Canaria.

Ricky: For a week, just sitting around?

Karl: Well there isn't much else to do on Gran Canaria. I mean I don't want to go slaggging the place off 'cos every time I talk about somewhere I seem to get into trouble for it.

Ricky: Yeah.

Karl: But, it's just like a big rock. It's volcanic, innit?

Ricky: You must have looked like a little barnacle on it.

Steve: Have you been there before?

Karl: I've been near it before – to another rock which was the same sort of thing.

Steve: If you've had your fingers burnt before, why did you go back?

Karl: Because you think they can't have loads of these islands that are the same – just a big rock with hotels on. They can't get away with it.

Steve: They obviously *are* getting away with it. Why do you keep going to these places that are just rocks? Why don't you investigate first? Ask your travel agent 'Is this a big rock?'

Karl : Because that's what you do, innit? You go and find out yourself. You take a risk and make up your own mind.

Ricky: What did you do?

Karl: It was just like one of them big hotels. That's where I made a mistake. It was one of those massive places where there's loads of people and you go for your dinner ...

Ricky: That describes a hotel. You've nailed that.

Steve: I've been to a few hotels myself – and that sounds like one.

Karl: D'you know what I mean though? There's the nice small ones where there's just enough people but this one's, like, mental. And it was full of old people really.

Steve: Sure.

Karl: That's probably why it's called Gran Canaria – 'cos there's ...

Steve: Grannies everywhere?

Karl: Yeah alright. But what what I thought I'd start doing is start a diary.

Steve: Okay. Why?

Karl: Just 'cos I sort of had a bit of time on my hands and that. I just thought 'write stuff down' and that.

Steve: Do you hope that this will one day become one the great literary works, like Samuel Pepys' diary?

Karl: I haven't heard of that. Is it any good?

Steve: You've never heard of Samuel Pepys' diary? The most famous diary in the world other than, perhaps, Anne Franks'.

Karl: I've heard of Anne Franks and that, and I thought if she's sat in a loft knocking stuff up with not much going on in her life at that point, yet she was still writing it down ...

Steve: Whereas you've been to Gran Canria, yeah.

Karl: Well I'm on holiday so I thought there is stuff going on that I can chat about so I'll start a diary.

Steve: Sure.

Ricky: You started a diary.

Karl: Yeah.

Ricky: And what are you going to do? Did you keep it up every day?

Karl: Yeah.

Ricky: Oh, can I read it please.

Karl: Well a diary's meant to be ...

Ricky: Please can I read it?

Karl: But some of it's only relevant to me it's sort of ...

Ricky: Oh Karl, please give me it.

Karl goes to get the diary. Ricky gets excited.

Ricky: Oh my god.

Karl returns with the diary

Ricky: Look how big it is!

Ricky and Steve laugh.

Ricky: It's huge.

Steve: It's one of those desk diaries.

Ricky: It's about a foot long. That is amazing. Imagine if
           Anne Franks' had been like that as she got it out.
           'Doof!' Everyone would have heard it clank down
           on the desk.

Karl: Yeah, but me writing's quite big, innit?

Ricky: Oh look. Give us that.

Ricky takes the diary.

Ricky: This is amazing.

Steve: Do you know about joined-up writing?

Karl: There's no point 'cos sometimes you can't read it can
           you?

Ricky: Oh my god. Look! It starts on the first day. This is
           wonderful.

Ricky reads from the diary ...

Ricky: *Going on 'oliday to Gran Canaria today. Woke up to the news that Tony Banks had died. There was a piece on the news about how everyone was shocked. Got me thinking about an invention that'd be good; a watch that counted down your life. If it says you've got three days left, go to the doctor's.*

Ricky and Steve laugh.

Ricky: *Told Suzanne about invention. She said she wouldn't buy one. But she said that about the iPod.*

Steve: How would this device work, this watch? How would you know when you are about to die? Is that a consideration? Or not something for you to worry about? Presumably the boffins would take of that.

Karl: No, all I was thinking was about that Tony Banks fella who died and everyone was shocked by it. But if you had a little watch on ...

Ricky: You can't just say 'wouldn't it be good'. How would this work? I imagine you're in the patent office going 'I've got an idea.' 'Certainly Mr Pilkington, what's your idea?' 'A watch that counts down your life.' 'Oohh, how does that work ...?'

Karl: Just pop it on your wrist.

Ricky: No no no. What do you mean 'just pop it on your wrist?' How does it work? 'Just pop it on your wrist.' Brilliant! You're an idiot.

Steve: Well it's interesting that he goes on ...

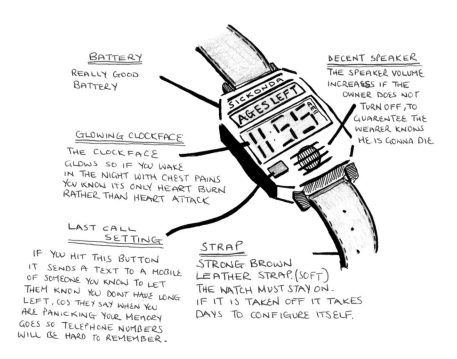

BATTERY

REALLY GOOD
BATTERY

DECENT SPEAKER

THE SPEAKER VOLUME
INCREAESS IF THE
OWNER DOES NOT
TURN OFF, TO
GUARENTEE THE
WEARER KNOWS
HE IS GONNA DIE

GLOWING CLOCKFACE

THE CLOCKFACE
GLOWS SO IF YOU WAKE
IN THE NIGHT WITH CHEST PAINS
YOU KNOW ITS ONLY HEART BURN
RATHER THAN HEART ATTACK

LAST CALL
SETTING

IF YOU HIT THIS BUTTON
IT SENDS A TEXT TO A MOBILE
OF SOMEONE YOU KNOW TO LET
THEM KNOW YOU DONT HAVE LONG
LEFT, COS THEY SAY WHEN YOU
ARE PANICKING YOUR MEMORY
GOES SO TELEPHONE NUMBERS
WILL BE HARD TO REMEMBER.

STRAP

STRONG BROWN
LEATHER STRAP. (SOFT)
THE WATCH MUST STAY ON.
IF IT IS TAKEN OFF IT TAKES
DAYS TO CONFIGURE ITSELF.

Steve reads from the diary ...

Steve: *The flight to Gran Canaria was a bit bumpy. I*
            thought about the clock that counts down your life
            again and I wondered if it would know if you're
            going to die in a disaster.

Steve: Now he's querying his own logic.

Ricky: He's wondering if it would know. He's invented this.

Steve: And now he's not even sure.

Ricky and Steve laugh.

Steve: *A fella on the plane was reading Koi mag. It was a fishing magazine. I glanced over and noticed he was reading the 'pond of the month' article. I don't think they could make it into a weekly magazine.*

Steve: Well to be fair to you I remember seeing a guy on a train once who was reading *Carp Monthly* – a magazine dedicated entirely to carp – and it had 'Carp of the Month'. And I thought, once you're about three months in the editor must be stressing. 'Have we got any more carp? Have we got a carp that's actually done anything?'

Ricky: I reckon if they used the same one twice there wouldn't be many complaints. 'That's the carp they used two years ago!'

Steve: *There was a really fat bloke on the plane. He was playing on his PSP. While I waited to go to the toilet I looked at what game he was playing. It was darts. He's that fat and lazy he can't even face playing a more active game on a games console.*

Me and Suzanne got off the coach with a couple of old people. One of 'em was in a wheelchair. I don't think it was wise of them to come to a volcanic island in a wheelchair. Everywhere's pretty rough paving and slopey. Guess I'll keep an eye on it as the week goes on. Day two in Gran Canaria ...

Ricky: Brilliant we're only at day two.

Steve: *The hotel is a bit odd. I've never seen so many cross-eyed people in one location.*

Ricky laughs.

Ricky: This is the best diary. This might be the best diary ever written.

Steve: *Whilst listening to The Kinks on my iPod, I wondered if everybody thinks in their own accent. I know I do.*

Steve: What's this? What you talking about?

Karl: When I was lying there sat on the lounger, right, and I was thinking about stuff ...

Ricky: How do you know you think in your accent? Tell me a typical thought.

Karl: Say if I was, like, if I saw something – do you know how I say 'that's a bit weird, innit?'

Ricky: But, when I think, I don't think the sentence like I'm saying it. It's just a thought. The thought appears; it's already there. It's not like I go, 'Rick?' 'What?' 'Just

215

looking over at that fella over there were ya?' 'I was, yeah.' 'I was thinking he looks a bit weird.' 'Oh, so was I.' I don't think out whole sentences.

Steve: Whereas you have 'Karl. Karl. Karl. Stop listening to The Kinks for a minute. Look over there. More cross-eyed people.' Is that how your mind works?

Karl: In a way, yeah.

Ricky: Brilliant.

Steve: That explains a lot.

Ricky: It's great that he has to think of whole sentences.

Karl: 'Cos I thought 'that's weird, innit'. I didn't think 'that's weird, isn't it?' and I thought, 'I actually think in me accent.' Then I thought, 'does Stephen Hawking – when he's doing his maths and that?' I don't know where he's from so I don't know what his accent would be like.

Ricky: I think he's from Kent or Cambridge or Oxford or something.

Steve: So you think he might think in that computurised voice?

Karl: Just wondered.

Steve: *Had lunch inside today due to shite weather. Sat next to an old fella. Old men's ears and noses carry on growing as they get older. Suzanne noticed his fingers were fat too. Maybe they continue to grow. Suzanne didn't laugh when I said her arse had the same problem.*

Cloudy start to the day. Had pie and chips in a cafe. Had an argument with Suzanne 'cos I thought it was daft that we were paying for food on an all-inclusive holiday. Changed my mind when I saw they sold pie though. The cafe was called Tattoo's. The fella who owns it didn't have any Tattoos. But we never saw his wife.

Ricky laughs.

Ricky: Brilliant.

Steve: *Had a drink in a bar. Everybody sat and watched one of the local cats lick its bollocks.*

Ricky is in hysterics.

Ricky: It's the greatest holiday in the world. That's the entertainment in that town.

Steve: *Went back to the hotel and had a sleep before tea.*

Steve: I love the fact that you're moaning about old people but you're just as bad.

Ricky: He's done nothing so far

Steve: He's done nothing and he's gone for a kip.

Steve: *Woke up to news about ducks being badly treated, there was a really ugly one with bent legs.*

Ricky: I'm gonna die. I'm gonna die. Why does he write this down?

Steve: *There is a fat bloke from Bolton who is in the pool as I write this. He's got a big tattoo on his back but I can't work out what it is ... he just got out of the pool and burped.*

Steve: Just felt like you had to keep us abreast of that.

Ricky: Everything's in the diary. I can see it getting to the point were you're going 'breathed in ... breathed out again.'

Steve: *There was a big fat fella in the sea who kept his t-shirt on. If you're big and fat, is there more chance of you getting burnt 'cos there is more of you on show? I asked Suzanne, and she said she didn't know in that sort of 'not listening' kind of way. I wanted to hang about to see if the fat fella was gonna get in the kayak but Suzanne said we had to head back.*

Ricky laughs.

Steve: *We go home today so we got up early to catch the last bit of cloud.*

Karl: No, it's just that it wasn't that sunny all the time. I mean, I was sat in weather that if it was like that here, there's no way I'd be sat in the garden.

Ricky: Yeah.

Karl: But 'cos you're on holiday you've got to sit in it. 'Put your coat on.'

Ricky laughs.

Steve: So are you going to continue to write this diary every single day?

Ricky: It's amazing. Keep this diary up! It's amazing.

Karl: I will keep it up 'cos what I find as well is, I think earlier on before I went away I think I did learn something, and because I wrote in down, I remembered it a bit better. So ...

Ricky: What was that?

Karl: ... I just was thinking then; I've forgot it now, but ...

Steve laughs.

Karl: But I remembered looking back at it and not having to read it all 'cos I remembered the end of it before I read it, if you know what I mean.

Steve: No. I have no idea what you are talking about.

Thursday

THERE'S AN ADVERT IN THE PAPER FOR A CIRCUS THAT IS COMING TO LONDON... IT HAS USED THAT IMAGE OF A BLOKE STICKIN HIS HEAD INTO A LIONS MOUTH....NOT THAT IMPRESIVE. IF HE DID THAT TO A LION WHILE HE WAS ON SAFARI I WOULD CLAP.

I LEARNT THAT IF YOU LINE UP ALL THE CHINESE PEOPLE IN THE WORLD, YOU WOULD NEVER GET TO THE END OF THE LINE IN YOUR LIFETIME.... I THINK THEY MEAN IF YOU ARE WALKING. THIS IS WHY CHINA IS DOING WELL IN THE BISINESS WORLD... MORE PEOPLE TO FLOG STUFF TO.

I PREDICT THAT THE ORIENTAL FLOWER SHOP ACROSS THE ROAD FROM THE FLAT WILL BE CLOSED BY THE SUMMER. I SAT LOOKIN OUT OF THE WINDOW TODAY AND ONLY ONE FELLA WENT IN.....AND THERE'S A SALE ON! THERE IS ANOTHER SHOP ROUND THE CORNER THAT JUST SELLS BUTTONS. I CANNOT SEE THE SHOP FROM MY WINDOW BUT IM GUESSING IT HAS BEEN JUST AS BUSY AS THE FLOWER SHOP TODAY.

GOING OUT FOR FOOD TONIGHT WITH GIRLFRIEND AND OTHER FRIENDS... .

DON'T KNOW WHAT I WANT TO EAT....GETTING BORED OF ALL THE FOOD ON OFFER.. I USED TO LOVE PASTA BUT IVE HAD ENOUGH OF IT NOW.

BACK FROM NIGHT OUT...HAD STEAK.... DIDN'T REALLY ENJOY THE FOOD BUT IT WAS CHEAP AS ANDY HAD VOUCHERS

JANUARY						
M		2	9	16	23	30
T		3	10	17	24	31
W		4	11	18	25	
T		5	12	19	26	
F		6	13	20	27	
S		7	14	21	28	
S	1	8	15	22	29	

GOT UP... WASHED UP.

I HAD A LOAD OF SOUP IN A PAN... DIDNT KNOW HOW TO GET RID OF IT SO POURED DOWN SINK. ME DAD SAID IT WOULD OF BEEN SAFE TO EAT. HE SAID ALL THESE USE BY DATES ARE A LOAD OF BOLLOX AND ARE ONLY CREATED BY SUPERMARKETS TO GET RID OF FOOD.

I WAS ABOOT TO TELL HIM ABOUT THE TIME I GOT BAD FOOD POISONING FROM EATING THE CAKES FROM ROOND THE BACK OF ██████████ BAKERY THAT THEY CHUCKED OUT BUT ME DAD CHANGED THE SUBJECT BY ASKING WHEN HE AND ME MAM WAS GONNA GET THERE CHRISTMAS PRESENT.

WENT TO GO AND GET SUZANNE'S SHOES FROM THE COBBLERS DOWNSTAIRS..... IT WAS £6 BUT I GAVE HIM £7. COULDN'T THINK OF ANY OTHER SHOPS WHERE I HAVE GIVEN A TIP.

TODAY I LEARNT ABOUT THE SAYING "BUSMANS HOLIDAY" IT MEANS PEOPLE WHO CONTINUE TO WORK EVEN WHEN THEY ARE OFF. IT COMES FROM THE FACT THAT THERE WAS A BLOKE WHO HAD A HORSE + CART AND DROVE PEOPLE ABOUT BUT WHEN HE HAD TIME OFF FROM DOING THE DRIVING HE WOULD SIT IN THE BACK WITH THE PASSENGERS WHILST A DIFFERENT BLOKE DID THE DRIVING. HE DID THIS COS HE DIDNT TRUST THE DRIVER TO LOOK AFTER HIS HORSE.

HORSES ARE HARD WORK. I DONT THINK PEOPLE SHOULD HAVE PETS THAT ARE BIGGER THAN THEMSELVES.

Saturday

GOING ON HOLIDAY TO GRAN CANERIA TODAY.

WOKE UP TO NEWS THAT TONY BANKS HAD DIED. THERE WAS A PIECE ON THE NEWS ABOUT HOW EVERYONE WAS SHOCKED. GOT ME THINKIN ABOUT AN INVENTION THAT WOULD BE GOOD. A WATCH THAT COUNTED DOWN YOUR LIFE....IF IT SAYS YOUVE GOT 3 DAYS LEFT.... GO TO DOCTORS.

TOLD SUZANNE ABOUT INVENTION... SHE SAID SHE WOULDNT BUY ONE.... BUT SHE SAID THAT ABOUT THE iPOD.

THE FLIGHT TO GRAN CANERIA WAS A BIT BUMPY.... I THOUGHT ABOUT THE CLOCK THAT COUNTS DOWN YOUR LIFE AGAIN AND WONDERED IF IT WOULD KNOW IF YOU WERE GONNA DIE IN A DISASTER.

THERE WAS A REALLY FAT BLOKE ON THE PLANE.. (HE GOT THE EMERGENCY EXIT SEAT...LIKE HE COULD JUMP UP QUICK AND OPEN THE DOOR! HE WOULD'VE HAVE PROBS GETTIN THROUGH THE DOOR) HE WAS PLAYING ON HIS PSP... WHILE I WAITED TO GO INTO TOILET I LOOKED AT WHAT GAME HE WAS PLAYING....IT WAS DARTS! HE'S THAT FAT + LAZY HE CANT EVEN FACE PLAYING A MORE ACTIVE GAME ON A GAMES CONSOLE.

ARRIVED SAFTLY AND SAT ON A COACH FOR ANOTHER HOUR TO GET TO HOTEL. THE WEATHER IS SHITE AND EVERYWHERE LOOKS PRETTY GRIM.

ME AND SUZANNE GOT OFF THE COACH ALONG WITH A COUPLE OF OLD PEOPLE. ONE OF EM WAS IN A WHEELCHAIR. I DON'T THINK IT WAS WISE OF EM TO COME TO A VOLCANIC ISLAND WITH A WHEELCHAIR (EVERYWHERE IS PRETTY ROUGH PAVING + SLOPY) GUESS ILL KEEP AN EYE ON IT AS THE WEEK GOES ON.

ANYWAY... GOT TO UNPACK AND BE IN FOOD HALL FOR 20:00.

FOOD WAS OKAY. FELLA ON RECEPTION TOOK THE PISS OUT OF ME BALD HEAD WHEN TELLIN US THERE IS ON SITE HAIRDRESSERS..... WHY DO PEOPLE TAKE THE PISS OUT OF ME BALD HEAD!

GOT BACK TO ROOM AND HAD A MESSAGE ON ME PHONE. IT TOOK TEN MINUTES FOR ME TO WORK OUT HOW TO ACCESS MESSAGES FROM ABROAD. IT WAS RICKY.

HE JUST LEFT A MESSAGE SAYING "ONE WEEKS HOLIDAY A YEAR MATE, THATS ALL I HAVE, THATS ALL YOU SHOULD HAVE MATE"

DAY 2 IN GRAN CANERIA.

THE HOTEL IS A BIT ODD. I HAVE NEVER SEEN SO MANY CROSS EYED PEOPLE IN ONE LOCATION.

THE SUN WAS OUT TODAY SO WE JUST SAT BY THE POOL.....AND READ.

I WAS READING A NEWSPAPER SUPPLEMENT THAT HAD A PIECE IN IT ABOUT THAT DRAG/TRANVESTITE BLOKE WHO WON THE TURNER PRIZE. STILL NONE THE WISER AS TO WHY THEY LIKE DRESSING UP LIKE THAT.

ALOT OF PEOPLE ARE STILL READING THE DE VINCI CODE. I DON'T THINK I COULD READ THAT AS I AINT REALLY READ THE BIBLE YET AND I THINK THAT THE DE VINCI CODE IS THE NEXT IN THE SERIES.

THE BLOKE ON THE SUN LOUNGER NEXT TO ME WAS READING 'TODAYS PILOT' MAGAZINE. THERE ARE SO MANY MAGS OUT ON SPECIALIST SUBJECTS! 'TO DAYS PILOT' FOR GODSAKE... NOT EVEN 'THIS WEEKS PILOT BUT TODAYS' DON'T THINK IT MUST SELL MANY. BEING A PILOT IS MEANT TO BE A STRESFULL JOB SO WHY WOULD YOU WANT TO READ ABOUT IT WHEN YOU ARE RELAXING FROM DOING IT.....DOCTORS/SURGEONS DON'T HAVE THEIR OWN MAGAZINES DO THEY?

A FELLA ON THE PLANE WAS READING 'KOI' MAG. IT WAS A FISHING MAGAZINE I GLANCED OVER AND NOTICED HE WAS READING THE 'POND OF THE MONTH.' ARTICLE.... DON'T THINK THEY COULD MAKE IT INTO A WEEKLY MAG.

WHILE SAT LISTENING TO 'THE KINKS' ON ME IPOD (SUNNY AFTERNOON) I WONDERED IF EVERYBODY THINKS IN THEIR ACCENT.... I DO.... I WONDERED IF STEPHEN HAWKING DOES.

HAD A WOLK TO THE SHOPS... LOTS OF TAT FOR SALE.
WENT IN ONE OF THE HOLIDAY SHOPS. WHY IS IT OKAY TO SELL DVDS ABOUT AVIN IT AWAY ASWELL AS POSTCARDS. THE SHOP WEAR WE GOT OUR CRISPS FROM HAD LIGHTERS NEXT TO THE CASH TILL WITH IMAGES OF WOMAN WITH NOWT ON...
                    WATCHED
GOT BACK TO HOTEL AND SAT ON BALCONY. AT THE HOTEL BEING BUILT ACROSS THE WAY... PLAYED FIND THE BUILDER WITH SUZANNE..... COULDN'T SEE ONE. THEY ARE TAKING THE PISS... THE WHOLE ISLAND IS ON ONE BIG HOLIDAY.

WENT FOR TEA, THE WOMAN FROM SCOTLAND WITH BLONDE SPIKEY HAIR WASN'T AS PISSED UP AS SHE WAS LAST NIGHT.

JANUARY					
M		2	9	16	23	30
T		3	10	17	24	31
W		4	11	18	25
T		5	12	19	26
F		6	13	20	27
S		7	14	21	28
S	1	8	15	22	29

Monday

WOKE UP TO NEWS ABOUT DUCKS BEING BADLY TREATED. THERE WAS
A REALLY UGLY ONE WITH BENT LEGS.

THAT ~~ABOUT~~ SONG THAT KIDS SONG 'THERE ONCE WAS AN UGLY DUCKLING' THE STORY
ABOUT AN UGLY DUCK THAT GREW TO BE A SWAN. I THINK THE STORY WOULD
OF WORKED ~~BETTER~~ IF THEY DID IT WITH A CATAPILLER COS THEY ARE PRETTY
ODD LOOKIN ~~THERE~~ BEFORE THEY TURN INTO A BUTTERFLY. (WONDER IF THEY MISS AVIN ALL
THE FEET)

ITS CLOUDY AGAIN..... BUT WE ARE SITTING OUTSIDE AGAIN! IF WE WERE
AT HOME AND THE WEATHER WAS LIKE THIS THERE IS NO WAY WE WOULD BE SAT
~~INSIDE~~ OUTSIDE.

THERE IS A FAT BLOKE FROM BOLTON WAY WHO IS IN THE POOL AS I WRITE
THIS. HE HAS A BIG TATOO ON HIS BACK BUT CANT WORK OUT WHAT IT IS DUE
TO ALL THE HAIR ON HIS BACK. IT LOOKS LIKE SOMEONE HAS DONE ONE OF THOSE
BRASS RUBBINGS ON HIS BACK.... HE JUST GOT OUT OF THE POOL AND BURPED.

WENT FOR A WEE. AN OLD BLOKE ON THE NEXT URINAL USED A DIFFERENT
APPROACH. HE WHIPPED OUT HIS NOB FROM THE TROUSER LEG RATHER THAN
THE TRADITIONAL 'OVER THE TOP' METHOD. HE DIDN'T SPEAK SO I DON'T KNOW
WHERE HE WAS FROM. HE DIDN'T WASH HIS HANDS EITHER.

IT WAS COLD SO WE WENT BACK TO ROOM AND WATCHED THE
WINTER OLYMPICS ON THE TELLY AS WE ONLY HAVE A CHOICE OF
SKY NEWS AND EUROSPORT AND SOME GERMAN CHANNEL. I WATCHED
THE LADIES SKELETON RACE. THIS IS WHERE A WOMAN SITS ON A TRAY
AND PUSHES HERSELF ON ICE. THINK SOME CANADIEN WON IT IN THE
END.

SAT ON BALCONY AND TRIED TO BLOCK OUT NOISY GERMANS NEXT
DOOR WHO WERE PLAYIN SCRABBLE.

A BOAT GOT STRANDED (ENGINE BROKE) PASSER BY'S STOPPED TO TAKE
PHOTOS AND VIDEO IT. A BIGGER BOAT WITH A GLASS BOTTOM WENT
OVER AND HELPED. EVERYONE ON THE BOAT CHEERED WHEN THE
PEOPLE WHO WERE STRANDED GOT ON BOARD. I DON'T KNOW WHY PEOPLE
BOTHER GOING ON THE BOAT TO LOOK AT THE ISLAND AS ITS NOT A NICE
LOOKING ISLAND. BLACK ROCK WITH HOTELS ON EVERY BIT OF SPARE LAND.
ITS JUST ONE BIG COUNCIL ESTATE SURROUNDED BY WATER.

RICKY CALLED..... SAME SHITE AS THE LAST FEW CALLS.... I LOST SIGNAL....
CALLED HIM BACK. HE THEN STARTED GOING ON ABOUT "OHH MATE,
YOU SHOULD ALWAYS GO TO PLACES WHERE YOU HAVE A STRONG SIGNAL
MATE... PEOPLE MIGHT NEED TO SPEAK TO YOU ABOUT WORK...."

CLOUDY START TO THE DAY.

WENT FOR BREAKFAST ON THE BALCONY AS IT WAS QUIET. PEOPLE WERE MOANING ABOUT THE TOASTER NOT BEING FAST ENOUGH.

WE DECIDED ON GOING FOR A WALK OUTSIDE THE HOTEL. IT WAS LESS A WALK... MORE AVOID TIMESHARE SELLERS.

HAD PIE AND CHIPS IN A CAFE. HAD A BIT OF AN ARGUMENT WITH SUZANNE COS I THOUGHT IT WAS DAFT THAT WE WERE PAYING FOR FOOD WHEN WE WERE ON AN ALL EXCLUSIVE... CHANGED MY MIND WHEN I SAW THEY SOLD PIE THOUGH. THE CAFE WAS CALLED "TATOOS" THE FELLA WHO OWNED IT DIDNT HAVE ANY TATOOS.... BUT WE NEVER SAW HIS WIFE....

WALKED BACK TO HOTEL... IT WAS TOUGH GOING BACK AS IT WAS ALL UP HILL.

THE SAME ACTIVITIES ARE GOING ON TODAY (STRETCHING/VOLLEYBALL/FOOTBALL). *COMEDY DANCING. WOMAN*ARE ON IN THE BAR TONIGHT... WELL GIVE IT A MISS.

JUST REALISED MY NEW YEARS RESOLUTION OF LEARNING SOMETHING EVERYDAY HAS GONE OUT THE WINDOW.. WILL TRY AND LEARN SOMETHING BEFORE THE END OF THE DAY.
        * (THURSDAY.) *
HAD LUNCH INSIDE TODAY DUE TO SHITE WEATHER. SAT NEXT TO OLD FELLA. OLD MENS EARS + NOSE CARRY ON GROWIN AS THEY GET OLDER. SUZANNE NOTICED HIS FINGERS WERE FAT TOO.... MAYBE THEY CONTINUE TO GROW. SUZANNE DIDNT LAUGH WHEN I SAID HER ARSE HAS SAME PROBLEM.

WE WENT FOR A GAME OF MINI GOLF. THE BLOKE IN THE HUT WAS A RIGHT MISERABLE BASTARD. (IT WASN'T MINI GOLF BUT CRAZY GOLF)

SUZANNE BEAT ME.... HAD A DRINK IN BAR... EVERYONE SAT AND WATCHED ONE OF THE LOCAL CATS LICK ITS BOLLOX.

WENT BACK TO HOTEL AND HAD SLEEP UNTIL TEA.

WOKE BEFORE TEA BY THE SOUND OF ME MOBILE RINGING. IT WAS RICKY SAYIN "YOU MUST BE AVIN A LOVELY TIME RELAXIN IN THE SUN, IM BUSY MATE ...WISH I HAD TIME FOR A HOLIDAY...."

Wednesday

GOT WOKEN UP BY SPANISH BUILDER DOIN SOME WORK NEXT DOOR. SUPPOSE HE HAD TO GET IT DONE SHARPISH SO HE COULD HAVE HIS SIESTA ON TIME. WOULDN'T WANT HIM TO LOSE ANY BLEEDIN SLEEP!

I GLANCED INTO THE ROOM AS WE LEFT OURS... HE WAS ONLY REPLACING A FEW BROKEN TILES.

TRIED TO RELAX ON SUN LOUNGER BUT KEPT BEING HASSLED BY THE REPS ASKIN ME IF I WANTED TO PLAY 'FOOTBALL' 'THEN VOLLEYBALL' STRETCHIN EXCEBIRI' TENNIS' "TABLETENNIS" "SWIMMING" "BASKETBALL".

WE DECIDED TO GO INTO THE SHOPPIN AREA TO GET OUT OF THE HOTEL AND GO. TO A PUB TO WATCH MAN UTD PLAY MAN CITY. THE BARS WERE ADVERTISING THE NIGHTS ENTERTAINMENT AND ASKING PEOPLE TO BUY TICKETS NOW AS THEY ARE GONNA SELL FAST. GOOD TO SEE 'SHOWADDYWADDY' IS STILL ATTRACTIN THE CROWDS.

WE WATCHED THE GAME. CITY WON 3-1.

WE MADE OUR WAY BACK. THERE WAS AN AMBULANCE LEAVIN OUR HOTEL AT HIGH SPEED. I RECKON THE REPS HAD GOT ONE OF THE O.A.P'S TO TAKE PART IN THE DECAFLON AND THEIR HEART CAVED IN. THE HOTEL IS FULL OF OLD PEOPLE. OLD BLOKES WITH SHORTS SHIRT AND TIE, SOCKS AND SANDELS.

WE SAT BY THE POOL AGAIN. I LISTENED IN TO THE FELLA WHO WAS READING THE PILOTS MAG THE OTHER DAY. HE WAS TELLIN SOME OTHER BLOKE HOW HE CAN NOW FLY A PLANE TO GREECE IF HE WANTED. ALL THE LESSONS WILL OF COST HIM 8 GRAND BY THE END.!!!!

HIS WIFE WAS A NURSE OF SOME SORT, SHE TOLD TOP GUNS WIFE SHE HAD TO ATTEND TO SOMEONE ON THE WAY HOME ON THEIR LAST HOLIDAY..."BLOOD PRESSURE PROBLEM" IF I WAS A DOCTOR I WOULD KEEP IT TO MESELF IF I WAS ON HOLIDAY... ESPECIALLY IN THIS HOTEL WITH ALL THESE OLD PEOPLE... NO WONDER ITS CALLED "GRAN" CANERIA.

THE OLD BLOKE TO THE LEFT OF SUZANNE STARTED SNORIN WHICH MEANT I COULDNT HEAR THE REST OF THE CHAT BETWEEN THE PILOT, NURSE AND OTHER COUPLE.

WENT BACK AND SAT ON BALCONY... THE NOISY GERMANS WERE OUT AGAIN. I THINK WE SHOULD GET RID OF ALL THE LANGUAGES... NO NEED FOR IT ANYMORE... THE WORLDS ALOT SMALLER THAN IT USED TO BE... AND WHILE WE ARE AT IT WE MAY ASWELL GET RID OF FLAGS.

WENT AND HAD TEA.

	JANUARY				
M	2	9	16	23	30
T	3	10	17	24	31
W	4	11	18	25	
T	5	12	19	26	
F	6	13	20	27	
S	7	14	21	28	
S	1	8	15	22	29

LAST FULL DAY IN GRAN CANERIA. MANAGED TO DO THE WHOLE WEEK WITHOUT GROUPING UP WITH OTHER HOLIDAY MAKERS.

HAD BREAKFAST AND WALKED DOWN TO BEACH (30 MINUTE WALK) IT WAS BUSY COS THE SUN WAS OUT. WE GOT A COUPLE OF DECK CHAIRS FOR 5 EUROS.

THERE WAS ALOAD OF PEOPLE IN WHEELCHAIRS DOWN NEAR THE ROCKS. THEY DIDNT GET CHARGED AS THEY STAYED IN THEIR CHAIRS...THOUGH THEY DID USE THE UMBERELLA. SO THEY FOUND A HOLE IN THE SYSTEM. AS THEY DIDNT PAY FOR IT.
THE CAREWORKER HAD STUCK A SWIRLY WIND THING AND FLAG ON ONE OF THE WHEELCHAIRS TO TRY AND CHEER UP THE FELLA SAT IN IT. THE CAREWORKER DIDN'T RELAX FOR MINUTE... SOME HOLIDAY IT IS FOR HIM. WHEELCHAIRS AND SAND DONT WORK WELL TOGETHER

WENT TO USE THE TOILET...IT COST 50 CENTS TO GET IN. THERE WAS A WOMAN SAT AT A DESK WITH TICKETS TO GET IN, ... SHE WAS DOIN PAPER WORK AND STUFF LIKE IT WAS A PROPER JOB. I DIDNT LIKE HAVIN HER SAT THERE AS IT FELT LIKE SHE WAS TIMING ME.

WALKED BACK TO DECK CHAIR THROUGH THE SHOPS. THEY WERE SELLIN THE USUAL TAT. TOWELS WITH THE MAP OF GRAN CANERIA ON. (NOT SURE WHEN YOU WOULD USE THAT) POSTCARDS, AND BOOKMARKS WITH PEOPLES NAMES ON, WITH A DESCRIPTION OF WHAT THAT PERSON TENDS TO BE LIKE. ALL OF EM SAID NICE THINGS...NOT ONE SAID 'THIS PERSON TENDS TO BE A TWAT' OR ANYTHING.

BOUGHT A COUPLE OF LOLLYS AND WENT BACK TO CHAIR.

I WAS A BIT BORED BUT WANTED TO GET A BIT MORE USAGE OUT OF THE CHAIRS AS IT HAD COST 5 EUROS...

THERE WAS A BIG FAT FELLA IN THE SEA WHO KEPT HIS T-SHIRT ON. IF YOU ARE BIG AND FAT IS THERE MORE CHANCE OF YOU GETTING BURNT COS THERE IS MORE OF YOU ON SHOW? I ASKED SUZANNE AND SHE SAID SHE DIDNT KNOW IN THAT NON LISTENING SORT OF WAY.

I WANTED TO HANG ABOUT TO SEE IF THE FAT BLOKE WAS GOING TO GET IN A KAYAK BUT SUZANNE SAID WE BEST HEAD BACK.

WE HAD OUR TEA OUTSIDE TONIGHT...WE SHOULD HAVE DONE THIS MORE OFTEN AS IT WAS NICE + QUIET

Friday

WE GO HOME TODAY SO GOT UP EARLY TO GET THE LAST BIT OF CLOUD!

ITS THE FIRST TIME WE HAD BEEN UP + ABOUT BEFORE 10AM. IT WAS CHAOS CHAOS... PEOPLE WERE PANICING THAT THEY WOULDN'T BE ABLE TO GET A NEWSPAPER...ITS FUNNY HOW PEOPLE MAKE HASSLE FOR THEMSELVES EVEN WHEN ON HOLIDAY.... ESPECIALLY THE OLDER PEOPLE.

WE GOT OUR USUAL CHAIRS... A NEW COUPLE SAT BESIDE US.... THE BLOKE HAD TATTOO'S ALL ON HIS ARMS + BACK. THEY WERE RELIGIOUS TYPE DRAWINGS. JESUS ON A CROSS ON HIS BACK... MARY HOLDING A BABY ON HIS ARM AND SOMEONE ELSE ON HIS ARM THAT WAS FURTHEST AWAY FROM ME. ITS ODD AS HE DIDNT LOOK LIKE A RELIGIOUS TYPE...IT WASN'T JUST THAT TATS THAT MADE ME THINK THAT.... IT WAS THE EARING AND SON'S ON HIS HAND.
HE ROLLED OVER SO HIS BACK WAS TOWARDS ME... UNDER THE CROSS WITH JESUS ON IT READ T·R·A·C·Y.

GONNA SIT + RELAX UNTIL 12... WEVE GOT TO BE OUT THE ROOM BY 12:30.

GOT HOME AT 12:30AM... TOO TIRED TO WRITE BUT THE FLIGHT WAS LONG AND ANNOYING WITH KIDS SCREAMING AND A WOMAN WITH A BIG HAIR DO STOOD IN FRONT OF THE TELLY.

JANUARY					
M		2	9	16	23	30
T		3	10	17	24	31
W		4	11	18	25	
T		5	12	19	26	
F		6	13	20	27	
S		7	14	21	28	
S	1	8	15	22	29	

That's that then. Hope you've enjoyed the book.

I think it was a good idea to put the Podcasts into book form as my accent isn't always easy to understand so it has made a lot of my points a lot clearer.

It's the best thing that I've ever put work into. Me Mam is well chuffed that I've got a book out. Me Dad will probably think it's not that good 'cos he likes *James Bond* books.

I'll use this space to say sorry to Suzanne that I have talked about her in the Podcasts and have said stuff about her hair and fat arse. But then people do say 'Write about what you know.'

I'm still doing the diary and doing more Podcasts so I hope you continue to listen to them and that.

KARL

The world record breaking
Ricky Gervais Show
podcasts come to CD

From the creators of The Office & Extras - The sensational podcasting phenomenon

3 CD set featuring:
- A brand new exclusive hour long show
- The best of the original series
- Over 3 hours of Ricky Gervais, Stephen Merchant & Karl Pilkington
- plus all 12 episodes of the original series in mp3 format

and keep up with the latest Podcasts at iTunes and Audible.com